Museums and Community

The community museum relationship has never been more important. It is seen as a primary responsibility of any museum to work with different communities, using collections to show people their histories, and also to encourage understanding outside that specific group.

This development of links between museums and communities is often taken for granted as a 'good thing' with little critiquing of the relationship and differing agenda present. Elizabeth Crooke argues that a much closer examination of the concept of community, and the significance of museums to different communities is needed, if the dynamics of the relationship are to be fully understood, and both sides are to get the most out of each other's resources. She uses research from across the social sciences, together with original work and a wide range of international case studies to illustrate her argument and provide pointers for the future.

The strongest focus is on areas such as Northern Ireland, South Africa, and North America. Here the politicisation of local populations highlights the complex issues faced by both museums and local groups, who have different ideas about what is appropriate and necessary in the museum context.

Elizabeth Crooke is Senior Lecturer in Museum and Heritage Studies at the University of Ulster.

Museum Meanings

Series editors

Eilean Hooper-Greenhill

Flora Kaplan

The museum has been constructed as a symbol in Western society since the Renaissance. This symbol is both complex and multi-layered, acting as a sign for domination and liberation, learning and leisure. As sites for exposition, through their collections, displays and buildings, museums mediate many of society's basic values. But these mediations are subject to contestation, and the museum can also be seen as a site for cultural politics. In post-colonial societies, museums have changed radically, reinventing themselves under pressure from many forces, which include new roles and functions for museums, economic rationalism and moves towards greater democratic access.

Museum Meanings analyses and explores the relationships between museums and their publics. 'Museums' are understood very broadly, to include art galleries, historic sites and historic houses. 'Relationships with publics' is also understood very broadly, including interactions with artefacts, exhibitions and architecture, which may be analysed from a range of theoretical perspectives. These include material culture studies, mass communication and media studies, learning theories and cultural studies. The analysis of the relationship of the museum to its publics shifts the emphasis from the museum as text, to studies grounded in the relationships of bodies and sites, identities and communities.

Also in this series:

Colonialism and the Object
Empire, Material Culture and the Museum
Edited by Tim Barringer
and Tom Flynn

Learning in the Museum
George Hein

Liberating Culture
*Cross-Cultural
Perspectives on Museums,
Curation and Heritage
Preservation*
Christina F. Kreps

Museum, Media, Message
Edited by Eilean Hooper-Greenhill

**Museums and the Interpretation
of Visual Culture**
Eilean Hooper-Greenhill

Museums, Society, Inequality
Edited by Richard Sandell

Past Beyond Memory
*Evolution, Museums,
Colonialism*
Tony Bennett

Re-Imagining the Museum Space
Beyond the Mausoleum
Andrea Witcomb

Reshaping Museums Space
Architecture, design, exhibitions
Edited by Suzanne MacLeod

Museums and Community

Ideas, Issues and Challenges

Elizabeth Crooke

Routledge
Taylor & Francis Group

LONDON AND NEW YORK

First published 2007
by Routledge
2 Park Square, Milton Park, Abingdon, Oxon, OX14 4RN

Simultaneously published in the USA and Canada
by Routledge
270 Madison Avenue, New York, NY 10016

Routledge is an imprint of the Taylor & Francis Group, an informa business

Typeset in Sabon by
RefineCatch Limited, Bungay, Suffolk
Printed and bound in Great Britain by
TJ International Ltd, Padstow, Cornwall

British Library Cataloguing in Publication Data
A catalogue record for this book is available from the British Library

Library of Congress Cataloging-in-Publication Data
Crooke, Elizabeth M., 1971–
    Museums and community : ideas, issues, and challenges / Elizabeth Crooke.
        p. cm.
    Includes bibliographical references and index.
    1. Museums—Social aspects.   2. Community life.
3. Museums—Social aspects—Case studies.   4. Community life—Case studies.
I. Title.
    AM7.C76 2008
    069—dc22
                                                                    2007021865

ISBN10: 0–415–33656–2 (hbk)
ISBN10: 0–415–33657–0 (pbk)
ISBN10: 0–203–37101–1 (ebk)

ISBN13: 978–0–415–33656–7 (hbk)
ISBN13: 978–0–415–33657–4 (pbk)
ISBN13: 978–0–203–37101–5 (ebk)

Contents

Figures

Tables

Acknowledgements

This book is the result of the friendship, advice and support of many people who have encouraged me with my interest in museums and my eagerness to explore their significance, and have led me to think more deeply about their purposes and influence.

After doctoral research at the University of Cambridge I joined the Department of Museum Studies, University of Leicester. I would like to thank those in Cambridge who encouraged my research and my colleagues in Leicester for expanding my thinking about the contemporary purpose of museums. Over lunches, between lectures, and during the occasional late night, we explored museums and their influence. I would particularly like to thank Ross Parry and Gerard Corsane who became good friends during my time in Leicester. I would also like to acknowledge the good humour and guidance of Simon Knell, which helped me through my first years of university teaching.

I will always be indebted to Brian Graham, his contribution to heritage studies, and the openings he created for its further investigation at the University of Ulster. This provided me with the opportunity for greater exploration of museums within the Irish context. Many of the ideas in this book were first explored in lectures on the Cultural Heritage and Museum Studies Masters programme at the University of Ulster. I would like to thank my students for their interest and contributions to that discussion.

A number of research trips have informed this study. I would like to thank Arts and Humanities Research Council (AHRC) Small Grants in the Creative and Performing Arts (ref. 12162) for support that enabled me to visit Cape Town in 2001. I am grateful to the Academy for Irish Cultural Heritages, University of Ulster, for funding research visits both locally and further afield. I would also like to acknowledge Edith Klein, Susan Solomon and Robin Ostow for the invitation to speak at the conference '(Re)visualising national history: museology and national identities in Europe in the new millennium', University of Toronto, in 2004. These research trips allowed me to share my ideas with colleagues and learn from their experiences.

Over the years many people have provided me with ideas, have answered my questions, and have made the completion of this book all the easier. In this regard, I would like to thank the following: the Crooke family, Chris Bailey, Bronagh Cleary, Pat Cooke, Briony Crozier, Patrica Davison, Margaret Edwards, Neal Garnham, Claire Hackett, Miriam Haddu, Robert Heslip, Michael Houlihan, colleagues at the International Centre for Culture and Heritage (University of Newcastle), Helen Lanigan Wood, Jane Leonard, the Levins family, Karen McCartney, Alan McCully, Sharon Macdonald, Madeline McGreevey, Linda McKenna, Hugh Maguire, Rhiannon Mason, Mark O'Neill, Johnston Price, Sandra Proslendis, Ciraj Rassool, Richard Sandell, Marie Louise Stig Sorensen, Kim Strickson, Lynne Teather, Gemma Thornton, and Leslie Witz. Ideas explored in this book have been introduced in some of my earlier publications and I am grateful to the editors and readers of those works for their comments.

I would like to thank the editors at Routledge for their patience while this project was completed – two periods of maternity interferes with deadlines. I am grateful to both Eilean Hooper Greenhill and Flora Kaplan for their support for this project. I am indebted to my referees who, at proposal stage, provided invaluable comments.

This book would not have been completed without the encouragement of my family. I am grateful to Ceallach Levins for his support and I dedicate this book to George and Patrick, and I thank them for being endless sources of delight.

Abbreviations

AAM	American Association of Museums
CDX	Community Development Exchange
CH	Cultural Heritage
clmg	Campaign for learning through museums and galleries
CRC	Community Relations Council
DCAL	Department of Culture, Arts and Leisure
DCMS	Department of Culture, Media and Sport
DENI	Department of Education for Northern Ireland
DWNMP	Dewsbury West Neighbourhood Management Pathfinder
EMU	Education for Mutual Understanding
GLLAM	Group for Large and Local Authority Museums
ICOM	International Council of Museums
IPPR	Institute for Public Policy Research
MA	Museums Association
MAGNI	Museums and Galleries, Northern Ireland
MLA	The Museums, Libraries and Archives Council
NEMLAC	North East Museums, Libraries and Archives Council
NIMC	Northern Ireland Museums Council
NMDC	National Museum Directors Council
OFMDFM	Office of the First Minister and Deputy First Minister
PAT	Policy Action Team
RCMG	Research Centre for Museums and Galleries
SAM	South African Museums
SACHM	South African Cultural History Museum
SMC	Scottish Museums Council
TSN	Targeting Social Need
UFTM	Ulster Folk and Transport Museum

Introduction

The complexity of museums as they are understood today is evident through the multiple readings of the museum space – readings that are taken within museums and imagined by those on the outside. Those who interpret museums are also diverse: men and women, majority and minority groups, able, disabled, academics, curators, visitors, non-visitors, adults, children. The people within these groups will also differ from each other, they will have widely divergent views, and each person will have a very personal sense of self and identity. It is this myriad that constitutes the museum's public; it is from this diversity that the museum must find its role, be relevant and seek value. The purpose of this book is to investigate the relationship between communities and museums and how museums work with communities. It is this symbiotic relationship that is at the centre of this study.

The links between museums, heritage and community are so complex that it is hard to distinguish which one leads the other – does heritage construct the community or does a community construct heritage? For many theorists, identifying community is about the recognition of shared characteristics, which are frequently grounded in an identifiable history, culture or landscape. Therefore, they would say that communities need a common base, provided by history, heritage or experience, in order to form. For those interested in the value of heritage and the promotion or establishment of museums, the importance of the past is dependent on those communities. In these instances it will be argued that communities construct heritage. When this debate is brought into the museum sector there is often discussion of the importance of communities to the future of museums. Community is presented as a means of advocacy that will, hopefully, ensure the relevance and sustainability of the museum. On the other hand, many will write about how museums help form community by expressing and representing community identities. This simple duality suggests that communities need the histories and identities preserved and interpreted in museums; and the museum sector needs the people, in the many communities, to recognise the value of museums and justify their presence.

The complexity of the relationship between community and heritage, as well as community and museums, is disguised by such a simple account. Instead, the links between the two are far more intricate and dependence too great to be able to say which needs the other more. Rather, community and its history, heritage and the museums we visit, are dependent on one another and, as this book will demonstrate, this dependence takes many forms. When we try to unpick these manifestations we must remember that ideas of how we define history, what is heritage and what form a museum should take will vary with the commentator. Similarly community is equally diverse, whether that is the community of people or community as an active agent representing needs and aspirations. For some, heritage is always a political term; it is seen as a construct that reflects the social and cultural needs of the people using and defining it. So too museums are products of their context – according to the time and place, they are ascribed with different purposes and meanings. Through the process of this book, by drawing on the vast range of debate and diverse examples of museum projects, I hope to unpick some of these issues.

Defining the study

Before I define the study I would like to explain what brought me to it in the first place, as this helps clarify the approach. At the beginning of my career of working in and with museums, and studying their meaning and impact, I was most fascinated by how they constructed and represented identity. My interest began with Ireland and how archaeology both as extant monuments and in collections was used to forge national identity in the nineteenth century. I enjoyed the myths and imaginings that grew up around monuments and precious artefacts and explored how people were encouraged to identify with collections and ascribe them with meaning that would subsequently shape social and political aspirations. Later, as a university lecturer, I was enticed away from the mystical round towers of the Irish landscape and towards current museum policy and the function of the contemporary museum. As my colleagues advocated that museums should make better connections with their communities, and be more aware of their social role, I found many of the issues that had occurred to me in my earlier studies were still relevant in contemporary critique. For me the practice of valuing heritage, interpreting material culture, building collections and creating museums all were a reflection of the social and political context. I felt that as we were being encouraged to consider museums' potential within the community, and as a means for community change, we should still ask whose agenda is being followed, what is the motivation behind creating the links, and what impact this is having on the representation of identities.

As well as these fundamental questions, which are also the subject of concern for many others within academic and museum circles, I was interested in the expressions of community heritage outside museums. While studying the construction of national identity in the nineteenth century I found it was just as valuable to consider what was happening beyond museums and how political figures, activists and individuals were selecting and promoting an idea of heritage relevant to their community. Here the selective processes revealed particular priorities. Heritage became a tool in their political process, and was used as an alternative means to promote a message. The attraction lay in the fact that 'the past' as heritage could be promoted as naturally occurring, unchanging, and part of tradition. If a political or social project could be built into heritage then it too could be presented as customary, predestined and part of a people's cultural heritage. In such cases, heritage could be used to increase the acceptability of politics and political projects.

Also, as we promoted a change in museum practice that takes greater account of communities I found that many community groups were 'doing museums', quite independently, in a fashion those inside the museum were advocating. After visiting a very successful community-based exhibition, produced in a community hall by a local group, temporarily mounted in an area well known to me, I asked myself why a community group would create their own display, with exhibition panels, display cases of artefacts and room reconstructions, and yet those members would rarely visit the local county museum. Had the museum, I wondered, with its good record in education and outreach, failed despite its best intentions? Or was it that on the surface the outcome looked quite similar (a museum-like exhibition) but if we could look back we would find that the processes were very different. Maybe what the community group was aiming to achieve through the process of creating the display and building the collection was quite different from the aims of the museum. Since those processes could not be achieved within the museum it would not be relevant for the community group to take an interest in the museum. Again, we need to ask what agendas are at play during the creation of community-based exhibitions. As we do so, developing an understanding of such processes is crucial to a better appreciation of the links between museums, heritage and community. It will reveal that no two community heritage initiatives are the same, no matter how similar the outcome, because the people and processes underpinning the activity will be different. The variations in context, time and place will give rise to different needs and aspirations that will shape the course of action.

In the midst of these concerns the meanings of museums and heritage will alter. The established museum, as it shifts its priorities and attempts to engage with new issues, will shift in meaning and relevance. The museum when fully integrated with a social or political agenda will be a different place from that which has greater distance from that influence. The community-based collection, exhibited periodically, will also have a different consequence and impact. Within this study I consider how the connection with community influences the meaning of museums, both when museums are a community construct and when they attempt to integrate themselves more fully with the needs of community. With regard to the latter, it is made clear that understanding community comes from a range of origins – it might be the needs as identified by government policy or those identified by the community leaders. In each case the approach and recommendations will differ. Unpicking those differences was one of the challenges of this study.

Because of the complexity of community and community agendas, this book brought me to territory that I didn't anticipate. I began with an interest in why community groups should create museums, and why museums might link with community, and found myself unpicking the meaning of community, the diversity of approaches to community development, and the political motivations underpinning community-based social movements. I had never before had the need to embrace so closely the literature of community studies, public policy or contemporary political theory, and I am certain I have only touched upon those areas. By doing so, I hope I have introduced some new perspectives into the debate on museums and community. This is also a highly selective study – there is great diversity in approaches to museums and communities and ways both can be investigated. There are also many examples of museum–community collaborations, each of which could be investigated for different purposes. In the case of this book, I have attempted to give a representative account of those links and illustrated them with examples of projects that I have found particularly illuminating. My own bias is on display here – particularly my interest in museums and heritage in Northern Ireland. I hope these examples appeal to you.

The structure of the book

The purpose of this study is to look more closely at the relationship between communities and museums and how museums work with communities to reveal the meanings raised by such connections. I have chosen to investigate a number of areas, each of which I have attempted to explore with very different examples of museum-based or related activity.

In order to put down the foundations for this study I felt it was important to investigate how we understand the two key themes of the book: museums and community. Within this my interest was to unpick the nature of museums and their links with community, both the links initiated by the museum and those forged by the community group. Secondly, it was very important for me to make the idea of community much clearer, especially with relation to its complexity as a concept and the range of ways community has been applied as an active tool. In relation to the latter I was most interested in its application as relevant to the museum, so my aim was to explore how community is symbolised, its role in public life, and how community can be part of social action. Chapter 1 considers why the notion of community can so easily be found in association with heritage, museums and display. There seems to be a natural appeal between the areas, which needs to be negotiated and explained. Two main strands of investigation run through the chapter: first the appeal of heritage and museums to community groups, both as a means of representation and exploration and to initiate change; and second, the rise of the notion of community as relevant to museum practices. Both of these strands have had influence on how we understand museums and on thinking about how they may evolve. Chapter 2 explores how community is understood and the different ways it has been considered and applied. It separates out the main uses of the idea of community: as a means of symbolising group identity; as part of public policy; and as a form of social action. The diverse approaches to understanding and investigating community can each be found reflected in how we understand museums. They are also to be found in methods of integrating an awareness of community needs into museum development, planning and policy. Understanding the nature of community group formation, and the features that enable its survival, is crucial to appreciating the role heritage awareness may play.

Community has become an integral part of public policy and I believe it is vital to get a better understanding of how this has influenced the museum. I have chosen to explore this area by analysing how community has become an important part of UK public policy and showing that, through its use by the government department responsible for culture, community has impacted on museum policy and planning. My desire is to reveal the origins of and approaches to many of the 'buzz words' of social policy, such as cohesion, inclusion and renewal, and their significance for museums. I want to identify the process by which government policy on community has impacted on the museum sector and explore how the nature of that policy is a consequence of political approach. Chapters 3 and 4 are linked in that they both consider community, museums and heritage in relation to the idea of community development. Chapter 3 outlines the rise of community concerns in UK-based cultural and museum policy. It refers to various national policies for community regeneration and the creation of the cohesive community, as well as the active and confident community, and demonstrates how this has been built into cultural policy, planning and initiatives. Specifically, examples from the museum sector will be used to reveal how the sector has adopted these policy concerns and has developed initiatives to respond to new demands – or is itself championing the potential link. Research and evaluation show, however, that greater consideration is needed when advocating the connection between culture and community development. This entails a better understanding of the purpose of community development as promoted through government; further questioning of the nature of the associations already made; and, maybe, even greater independence between the cultural sector and government. Chapter 4 is an opportunity to dig deeper into the idea of social capital, which is so often being linked with community projects in the cultural sector. A particular idea of community is central to social capital, and how this can be exercised in relation to museums and culture is explored through the example of the Museums and Community Initiative, led by the American Association of Museums. Chapters 5 and 6 provide a greater focus on community relations practice. This is explored in Chapter 5 through the ideas of cultural diversity and multiculturalism and how these have impacted on museum practice. Chapter 6 looks particularly to Northern Ireland. Because of the impact of the conflict in and around Northern Ireland, community relations are an everyday concern and have been used to inform working practices in schools, museums, the health sector and each tier of government.

An important aspect of this study was to look at some of the ways that community groups have used heritage. This is a theme in Chapter 1, in which I refer to the importance of objects and collections as a means for a community to represent itself, both to its own members and to those on the outside. This theme

is returned to in Chapter 7 and runs through the analysis of community movements and my consideration of how and why museum display is a means to
achieve the goals of such movements. Three examples of heritage projects, which
link with different forms of community movement, were chosen: the first an
education movement, the second conscientisation, and the third empowerment.
Together they reveal the museum as a powerful tool to achieve the goals of
community, as defined at the grass roots.

Together, each of these chapters brings a different perspective to what is community, and how it might function. As well as that, each of these perspectives
provides different purposes for museums and heritage. The multiple meanings of
community and museums come together in the museum as an intersecting space
or 'contact zone'. The idea of the museum as a place with multiple meanings is
the theme of the final chapter, which uses the exploration of community as a
means to answer the 'why museums' question. There are many perspectives on
the issue of why we have museums, as well as their roles, impacts and meanings.
Each of the perspectives on community had a different relationship with the
museum, revealing separate and discrete understandings of the connections.
What can happen when these perspectives come into contact and intersect with
each other is potentially the most interesting aspect. On the one hand, that
intersection may be an opportunity for innovation; on the other, it could have
unstable and volatile results.

1

The appeal of community, museums and heritage

Community heritage is a notion that is referred to so often and so effortlessly that one might consider it unhelpful to unpick the association – over-analysis might cause the essence of the relationship to be lost when the pieces are pulled apart and considered individually. That is not the goal of this chapter; instead, its purpose is to explore that relationship, to reveal the nature of the connections, and to discover why the two so often come together. The chapter uses recent experiences of how community has been associated with heritage, museums and display to demonstrate the appeal of one for the other.

This chapter begins with a consideration of why the idea of community has been integrated with museums and heritage, both by people inside the museum and by groups who independently pursue heritage and museum projects. With regard to the former, community is shaping museum initiatives; with regard to the latter, museum activity is a means to express community identity. It is the contribution of museums to identity that is the theme of the second section. Since the beginning of museums, their display, architecture and presence have been a means to communicate the identity of the place and people at their core. The third section looks to how a greater awareness of community and community concerns has influenced museum practice, ranging from the types of exhibitions mounted, to the development and management of collections, as well as staffing and new programmes in museums. The closing section looks to how these various aspects of how museums and community have come together have caused us to rethink what a museum is and what its potential might be. As a contribution to this study this chapter lays the foundation of the appeal between museums and community that is the basis for many of the initiatives explored in later chapters.

The currency of community

In museum and heritage studies, community has been considered in numerous ways, from involving the people whose histories and cultures have inspired the formation of collections through to developing an awareness of the shared responses of people to exhibitions and collections. There is now increased use of the phrase 'community museology'[1] and greater knowledge of the complexity of museum audiences. On the ground we can consider the relationship between museums, heritage and community in two ways. First, we can look to the rise of community within the official museum sector, which can be considered as the professional museum sector such as advisory bodies, central or local government funded museums, or private museums with accredited status. This would include museums that are adopting professional standards of best practice and which have or seek the status of such museums. These institutions are more likely to follow the recommendations of professional bodies and to be influenced by government policy. Following on from the rise in profile of policy relating to community, it is now commonplace for museums to appoint a community outreach officer, or at least to have a member of staff with that responsibility. Often such museums have community galleries, may mount exhibitions targeted at specific community groups or, indeed, may have developed a community policy. Many of the established, state-run and 'official' museums are willingly involved in community activity, be it community consultation or working with communities on exhibitions; or they may take seriously the impact they may have on their community. Museums Australia, for instance, advocates the formation of 'community collections', informed by 'the keepers of community knowledge'.[2] In the US the Museums and Community Initiative, led by the American Association of Museums, was used as a means to gather information about how communities regarded museums and to develop a 'toolkit' that would enable museum staff to work better with the community.[3] We should remember that within the official museum sector there is great diversity. In the UK, for instance, we should distinguish between national and local authority museums, each of which will have a very different history, mission and relationship with its public. In relation to the issues of governance, national museums are centrally funded and their public is across the UK, with pronounced diversity. The future of these museums is closely tied to central government policy, and as attitudes in government shift so too will priorities for the department funding these museums. Local authority museums, run by local, district or city councils, are often closer to a specific geographical electorate, and in order to continue to receive political support they are aware that they need to reach as wide an audience as possible. As a result they may find it easier to get a clearer sense of who their communities are, the nature of those communities, and how best to respond to their needs.[4]

The second area to consider is the interest in heritage and museum activity emerging from the communities themselves, and we can refer to this as the 'unofficial' museum sector. Community groups, often with no museum training and little care for standards of museum practice (such as how best to write a text panel), often produce the most interesting, passionate and relevant exhibitions or collections reflecting their own experiences and priorities. In most cases, this community–heritage engagement has not been triggered by policy guidelines or recommendations; instead, it comes from members of the community and is inspired by their own perceptions of what they need and how this can best be achieved. There are other characteristics of this form of community heritage initiative: they are sometimes transient, often personality led, and frequently only best used and known amongst the community from which they emerged. They are often highly independent and subject to a different form of scrutiny. Rather than being guided, monitored and even restricted by professional museum standards, expectations and the glare of peers, it is more likely that this form of governance will come from within the community itself. Therefore, community initiatives will develop reflecting the community, as defined by its leaders, incorporating its strengths, as well as weaknesses. The less attractive characteristics of community may not be escaped: its exclusiveness, the boundaries, and its limits. Some of this will be related to why a community interests itself in heritage. Rarely will a community group participate in heritage without reason: there are often distinct motivations behind such activity that reflect the needs and aspirations of the community. Collecting oral histories, the creation of exhibitions and the formation of local history groups will often be drawn into the pursuit of other goals that can be social, economic or political.

Although, for ease of understanding, I have presented two forms of community heritage, in reality it is far more complex than that. It is also the case that a community heritage initiative, emerging from the unofficial sector, can, when longer established, take on the characteristics of the official sector. Over time, a community initiative may well become more closely involved with the established heritage sector, maybe by adopting professional standards or linking with policy initiatives emerging from the sector. Or the established heritage sector may well support a community initiative, and be prepared to keep its distance, so allowing the initiative to emerge independently. It is also the case that the idea of a community museum differs in different contexts. In the UK the Leicestershire County Council Community Museums Strategy, for instance, has been set in place to support voluntary and independent museums in the region. Most of these receive no regular funding, are run by volunteers and are very closely linked to the local communities. Many relate to local historical societies and exist due to the enthusiasm of a few key members. Leicestershire County Council has appointed a Community Museums Officer who, with a grant budget, aims to support these museums in the areas of standards, audience development, sustainability and learning.[5] A similar concern for introducing standards to the independent museum sector is found in Canada and is illustrated by the 'Standards for Community Museums' initiative in Ontario[6] or the 'Community Museums Assistance Program' in Nova Scotia.[7] In these examples the majority of community museums are local and independent and have been established to communicate the history of the area and the passions of local individuals.

This differs very greatly from the idea of a community museum or centre that has grown popular in Australia or South Africa, for example, where they have been developed with far more radical and social agendas in mind. Moira Simpson discusses the use of museums amongst Australian Aboriginal communities. These museums, she writes, may incorporate aspects of conventional museums, but they are used to counteract traditional museology by omitting or including activities or methods important for their local agendas. In the Aboriginal context this may be a means to protect their communities from intrusion – the museum becomes a 'tourist stage' – or to assert cultural autonomy. The museum may be a means to articulate social and political concerns, contest official histories, and present alternative narratives. It may also act as a form of education and reconciliation between different peoples.[8] These museums, by being closely linked with community objectives, can also be identified as political spaces. Davalos, for instance, describes examples of the formation of community museums in the US resulting from a sense of exclusion and as a form of resistance. As advocates for ethnic communities, these museums are often directly involved in community development, political action and protest.[9] In their description of new museums in South Africa, Mpumlwana *et al.* refer to them as community resources engaged with the goal of political democratiz-ation.[10] Community can also be taken as an example of the politicisation of the museum and, as noted by Karp,[11] this can raise acute moral dilemmas. At times community heritage may result in requests that are oppressive to another com-munity. A group may have a very exclusive idea of how to represent their particular community, which rejects certain members or expressions of local identity. Such cases will encourage us to ask who is speaking for community and why, and to ascertain whether all demands made by community in relation to heritage are equally valid.

A museum that straddled the idea of a museum originating from established practices, but attempting to take on a more radical agenda, is that of the example of the Anacostia Museum Columbia and its history reveals the tensions that can arise from these different perspectives. The museum was established in 1967 in one of the poorest areas of the District of Columbia and, although always linked to the Smithsonian Institution, in its original format the museum was very much a community initiative that was well connected with the local African American community.[12] In her account of its history, Portia James described the museum as having developed along its own independent lines, quite different from many official museums at the time: it involved local community activists and leaders; informal advisory groups were populated by local groups; and management structures were kept simple: 'there were no curatorial or research personnel and, initially, no departments'. In the early years, an individual identity, separate from the Smithsonian, was deliberately maintained. James describes local community members as regarding the museum as a means to share 'their insights, their perspectives and their history', and their interest as inverting the Smithsonian's original mission in order to suit their needs.[13] However, with time, the museum entered a new phase triggered by the professionalisation of its activity. This phase saw a reduction of participation by community members, the museum moving away from a relatively busy area and into a nearby park, and more sophisticated and costly exhibitions. Maybe most revealing was a change of name that dropped the word 'neighborhood'. In James's account, mainstreaming the museum 'weakened the museum's structural ties to the community it served'.[14]

The example of Anacostia Museum raises important questions for those interested in the relationship between museums, heritage and community. Heritage has multiple purposes and the motivations for participation in heritage activity will differ according to one's position in relation to it. There will also be numerous interpretations of the function, impact and success of various projects and how those might be measured and valued. The community group might regard a short-term heritage project, perhaps a collection that has been brought together for a short period, as a success. A professional museum curator, in contrast, might judge success on longevity and permanence. There are many different ways of 'doing' museums and heritage, and one judgement on what is appropriate will often be different from another. Sometimes, concern with the professionalisation of collecting or exhibiting practices may well be missing the point of the community initiative. I experienced this when I visited the museum in the Apprentice Boys Memorial Hall, Northern Ireland, along with a group of people that included a local museum curator who was well aware of best practice in collections care, display and handling.

The Apprentice Boys is a members-based group that was established in the early nineteenth century to mark the Siege of Derry in the 1680s. The collection on display was formed by a member of the organisation and is held in one of the most important meeting rooms within the Memorial Hall. Over the years the museum has become a disparate collection of artefacts, some of which are related to the social and political history of the locality while other items simply make up a most bizarre cabinet of curiosities. In the summer the museum is open to the public one day a week and some of the most historically important objects within the collection are on open display, for visitors to handle (see Figs. 1.1 and 1.2). Documentation of the collection is minimal and concern for collection care issues in little evidence. For the professionally trained curator amongst my group this was anathema and, indeed, made his visit very uncomfortable. Although I have great respect for the best of museum standards, in this case their adoption was not the primary concern of the collector and would perhaps contravene the aims of the collection. If it was suggested that the collections should be moved to the nearby city council museum, which employs high standards of collections care and display, this would lessen the value and meaning of the collection for the local community group. The fact that community members, who care greatly about the history of their local area, can regularly and easily handle items dating from the Siege and later historical events is important, and the ability to hold local meetings in the community hall, amongst the artefacts that inspire the group, is of immense value. For this group the material culture in context is a means to construct community identity and form bonds between members, both past and present. The objects are the tangible link between imagined communities – they are the link to people the members can never meet.

Museums and formation of identity

Whether one's interest is increasing the profile of community within the official museum sector or understanding better the role of heritage in community-led initiatives, one can sense a re-evaluation of how museums are defined and engaged with. Museums are no longer only being established in imitation of the

Figure 1.1 The Apprentice Boys Museum, Apprentice Boys Memorial Hall, Londonderry, 2006

grand Louvre or Hermitage expression of a museum as high culture, created in the eighteenth century. Instead, the broader concept of the folk, eco or living museum is gaining popularity. This early idea of a museum and its collection was born from activity of the elite: vast collections were created by royalty and the upper classes, packed with the products of the Grand Tour. These were the hobby museums that became the pastimes of the leisured classes. Recent research into the history of collecting in nineteenth-century England has shown how an interest in developing natural history and antiquarian collections occupied the minds of these men. It is these people whom we should acknowledge for the wealth of many of the county museums as well as the national collections in the London capital. In Scotland and Ireland a similar tradition also emerged, with gentlemen's clubs forming the early collections of the Scottish Antiquaries Museum and the Royal Museum of Edinburgh, now part of the National

Figure 1.2 The Apprentice Boys Museum, Apprentice Boys Memorial Hall, Londonderry, 2006

Museums of Scotland, and the Dublin Museum of Science and Art, renamed the National Museum of Ireland early in the twentieth century. Still today collecting is a popular activity, although its expression may not be so recognisable to the collectors of the past. A new form of contemporary collecting has emerged outside museums. This is not the art and archaeology found in the museums we may frequent; today's collectors include those who are occupied with building collections of ephemera – be it packaging, badges or posters.

Museums are not only about the collections they house – they are also about the sense of the past they represent. Museums symbolise culture, identity and heritage. For new nations the story told in museums by the objects on display can endorse a political message, and can give a tangible link to a frequently elusive concept. The method by which nationalism has employed museums reveals much about how they hold their significance. An aspect on which the many theories of nationalism agree is that a sense of 'the past' plays an important role in fostering national identity. According to how one understands nationalism, this past may be one that is reinterpreted, revived, invented or imagined. In each case, however, references to past events and heroes are used to unite the people around the idea of the nation and as evidence of a glorious past and national achievements. The past is an essential component of ethnic myths that forge nations: it provides a sense of antiquity and ancestry; aids the definition of a sense of place; and can be used to represent the golden age.[15] Even more so, the material remains of the past preserved in national museums provide an indisputable link to this glorious past. Chosen objects can authenticate the nation, provide inspiration for the future and legitimise present-day aspirations. Moreover, the very nature of museums and how they are valued contributes to this process. It is for these reasons that collections and museums were formed at the height of national movements throughout Europe in the nineteenth century, such as the Hungarian National Museum in Pest and the National Museum of Prague in Central Europe,[16] as well as public museums in Greece, Spain and Denmark.[17] This influence can also be found in nineteenth-century Ireland. From early in the century, political leaders and writers in favour of an independent Ireland referred to archaeological sites and objects as evidence in support of their aspirations. In the same period, the collectors, and those in Ireland interested in the creation of a public museum, were well aware of how their activity related to the national sentiment and politics of the day. For both, the identity of the emerging museum was important. This is reflected in heated debates on the nationality of the architect of the Dublin Museum, the use of space, the choice of artefacts for display, and even the title of the museum. Early on in the Museum's history these aspects reflected its links with the Department of Science and Art in London. Later, in the new century, with its reinvention as the 'National Museum of Ireland', and subsequent changes in display, the new museum became representative of independent Ireland.[18]

This sense of representation is just as relevant today as it was in the nineteenth century. Indeed, using the study of nationalism as a means to understanding museums reveals important aspects of their significance. The values that made museums useful for nationalism are the same characteristics that give them relevance today. Although the collections that we form today may be very different from those created by our predecessors in the eighteenth and nineteenth centuries, the reasons why we collect are much the same. Today, as in the past, collections are an expression of our identity.[19] As we build collections they become an extension of ourselves; they reflect what we are interested in, our values and our judgements. Collecting historic objects may appear to be about looking back, but very often it can be a concern about looking forward. Collections may be formed on the grounds of nostalgia or aspirations. People collect for themselves and for others. Collectors, displaying items in their home or donating publicly to a museum, are telling other people something about themselves. Their personality is revealed through the collection. Collecting for others may also take the form of preserving memorabilia of a group of people, be it a local church, those connected through place, or a community of people who share particular history or experiences. Such examples reveal that at both the local and the national level, museums and community must be considered in relation to issues of identity, representation and the role museums have in constructing a sense of place, belonging and self. Furthermore, cultural participation, whether it is heritage, arts or museum projects, is a social context within which identity development can take place. Lowe, in a study of art and community development in Denver, discussed how participation in arts projects allowed people to develop their self-perception at both individual and group level.[20] In this instance, arts projects developed a greater sense of self-awareness, provided opportunities for self-expression and enhanced self-esteem. Shared experiences through group participation allowed people to communicate and to exchange experiences, values and understanding that forged links and group identities. Cultural activity, whether through participation in the arts or through the formation of collections and display, must be read in the context of these forms of identity formation. Museums and heritage can impact on the formation and representation of identity and we can construct and explore our identity through cultural participation.

Communities engaging with heritage

It is these issues of identity and representation that are often at the core of community-led heritage initiatives. Frequently, these are grass-roots initiatives developed by people who are non-experts in the practice of heritage or museum management, but who are well aware of the value and significance of the heritage around them and its potential. Many in the museum sector are advocating that the museum concept be revisited, and indeed some museum services have embraced the idea of transforming the museum. If we look beyond the official heritage sector to find out how people not concerned with the usual practices of museums have engaged with the ideas of collecting, interpretation and display, further examples of originality can be found. Maybe these groups are engaging with heritage in a way that museum professionals, in favour of transforming the museum, can only aspire to. Many in museums refer to the need to connect with communities, create community collections, and be deeply involved with social, welfare and developmental issues. Proponents support a grass-roots approach that is more relevant and acceptable. Some will go so far as to advocate a service that has its objectives set by the community, on its own terms. Often the best examples of this already happening are the community groups who are creating their own separate heritage initiatives that relate to their current needs, interests or welfare concerns. These initiatives are very much connected with the grass roots, emerging with local community leaders and participants. Again, the nature of community-led heritage will reflect the social, political and economic context and, although I may refer to it as being independent from the official heritage sector, the initiatives are not independent from influence. This influence will be that of the community itself, and its particular agendas. Furthermore, many grass-roots community heritage initiatives will seek financial or advisory support from institutions linked to national or central government. This often means they have to incorporate the most recent trends in state policy in their initial application and then report on the initiative's contributions to these areas.

What is undeniable is the enthusiasm of local historical societies and community groups who use their local heritage as an anchor for other activities. In the UK, Community Development Associations have formed in rural and urban areas when people have become increasingly aware of the challenges facing younger people, rising unemployment, and experiences of exclusion. Members of such associations engage in various activities that promote local businesses, tourism, youth work and the needs of women.[21] One such is a network formed in Northern Ireland to support community regeneration – the area experienced high deprivation and poor access to resources. As part of a wider strategy of community networking, relationship building and training, a Heritage Audit was launched in 2004 as a means to develop a reservoir of information about the natural, cultural and built environment. Local community groups and primary schools are producing heritage maps, which include features of importance to their local community, enriched with personal photographs, pictures and stories. The maps are thought to be an important means to develop pride in the area and make connections between people and generations.[22] This Audit is also regarded as an important contribution to the overall task of regenerating the area. This is an example of how heritage is an important activity outside the museum and cultural sector and has relevance for developmental and community-based initiatives. This can also be seen in the two examples that follow. One is a single local initiative and the other a museum network; both illustrate how community history projects can, in unexpected ways, become so much more.

In Londonderry, Northern Ireland's second largest city, women have come together to form a group called 'Women into Irish History'.[23] As well as setting up lectures on local history, the group has toured local and national historical sites, including a visit to France and Belgium as part of their desire to learn more about the First World War. The impact of these activities is revealed in a publication, written by the women, which is an accessible description of their local history and their experiences learning about it. The book is intended for other women in a similar position to themselves, who are also interested in history but find the usual channels to learning more about it no longer available or simply unsuitable. As well as that, the publication is a biographical account that reveals as much about the women's experiences growing up in Derry, and how they identify with their local history, as it does about the sites the group visited. A Protestant woman was happy to write that she thought she 'knew everything about [her] culture', but now feels she has so much more to learn. Another told how as a child she played by the city Workhouse, which was still in use in the late 1940s. She called the people inside paupers, without knowing what the word meant; she now visits their graves. A woman from a Nationalist background provided a moving account of visiting the site of the Battle of the Somme and her feeling that, as a Catholic, she should not be going – since her visit she says a prayer on Remembrance Day for those who died. The motivation behind the formation of Women into Irish History was to learn more about history. Because it was a group from mixed backgrounds it also became about forming an understanding of shared culture that might contribute to 'building a better future for everyone'.[24] The members of the group made new friends and took part in activities they had little opportunity to do in the past. They were also able to publish a record of their experiences, something they never imagined at the outset. The engagement with history experienced by the group had far greater consequences and meaning than simply having a better knowledge of historical events – it also had an impact on how the women made sense of that history, of how they related to it in the present, and what it means for them in the future.

In the State of Oaxaca, south-east Mexico, a community-based cooperative has developed a network of local museums as part of a range of projects with the aim to contribute to social and economic improvement of their area. Inspired by the importance of the cultural heritage of the region, and encouraged by the interest of anthropologists working in the area, as well as the financial support of development agencies, the idea of the *museo comunitario* network was born, described as 'a bottom-up community museum networking process'. The opening of the first museum in the mid-1980s has led to the creation of ninety-four community museums in seventeen Mexican states. The network is seen as an example of how development can have a positive impact on the mobilisation of social capital, empowerment of the rural poor, enhancement of local government, the creation of durable partnerships between the state and civil society, and the creation of local defences against the homogenising forces of cultural globalisation.[25] In his account of the project Healy praises the 'bottom-up' approach to this museum network as having been essential to its success. This project is seen as a positive alternative to other 'misdirected' community museum programmes in which 'a top-down leadership and management style have left community members on the outside looking in rather than vice versa'.[26] Community members describe *museo comunitario* as a means to developing a greater sense of collective ownership and raising self-esteem. One member stated how before his involvement with *museo comunitario* he had had a 'vague notion' of his cultural roots and had 'felt ashamed', but 'now my knowledge and pride in my cultural origins have given me an empowering sense of cultural identity'.[27]

The broad approaches to museums and heritage, taken by the community groups described above, reflect the essence of the idea of the ecomuseum. The ecomuseum is a concept that focuses on place and looks beyond the walls of the museum to nurture cultural, natural and built heritage as interlinked and interdependent. Founders of the concept were concerned with the democratisation of the museum and felt that by seeing the museum as part of the landscape it would be closer to local communities. The idea emphasises the point that fieldscapes, archaeological sites and historic buildings should not only be valued individually, but should also be thought of collectively, as a network, preserved together and in relation to each other. Accordingly, we should preserve not only the landscape, but also the folklore attached to it. Not only the archaeological sites, but also the artefacts associated with them. Not only the prized buildings in a town or village, but also other town features that give those buildings their meaning and context. Many of those writing on the approach, such as

Peter Davis, argue that because the ecomuseum is based in the community it has greater potential for empowerment and is a more effective use of heritages.[28]

These examples emphasise the passions raised and connections made by community-based heritage initiatives. The projects are part of a journey, which in these cases the people have made both as individuals and as part of a group. In such cases heritage becomes a carrier – a process that takes on a range of meanings, brings people together, and will move them both physically and emotionally. Sometimes the concern can be locally based, other times the impact and issues can take on national or international dimensions. Regardless of scale, community heritage experiences can be very powerful and, at the best of times, can inspire positive personal development and community change. While celebrating the best achievements we must be sensitive to a range of possible outcomes and experiences.

Material culture of community

The accounts of how community groups have engaged with their local history, whether that is because of personal or social interests, as demonstrated by the Apprentice Boys collection, or because of a community development agenda, as demonstrated in Oaxaca, show how the material heritage has taken on additional significance and resonance. In each case the material heritage was given particular purpose that reflected the needs of the group. The meanings associated with the material heritage altered as people's relationship with the history it represented changed. As our sense of who we are, how we relate to others and what we are capable of doing shifts, the objects that are part of that exploration take on additional meanings and consequence. This is well demonstrated in the work of archaeologist Sian Jones, who has investigated the meanings associated with an early medieval monument for a rural community in Scotland. The monument is a *c*.800 AD cross-slab located in the village of Hilton of Cadboll.[29] Part of the monument is on display in the Museum of Scotland in Edinburgh and a second part (as well as a reconstruction of the entire monument) is in the village. Village members, interviewed by Jones, refer to the monument as a 'living member of their community' and 'an ancient member of their village'. The monument is considered as having been born in the area, growing amongst the community and having soul, charisma and feelings. There is also a sense, if the monument is threatened, of the community dying.[30]

The example of the cross-slab of Hilton of Cadboll illustrates very well how material heritage can become part of the culture of a place or of a community. Artefacts can become a means to express the needs of the local people and their concerns about preserving local identities. They can also be a means to express reaction to external processes or threats. At times this may not be an entirely planned action; instead, the artefacts by being integrated within the community become part of the community experience. For others the very development of a heritage dimension to their work can be a conscious reaction and a deliberate means to communicate a message. In these cases it is not the heritage that is of value; instead, it's what heritage can say about the community group that is of greatest importance.

Some of these issues are raised by the display of Orange Order artefacts in Northern Ireland. The Orange Order is a member-based organisation founded in Ireland in the 1790s as a means to mark the victory of Protestant King William III over Catholic King James II in a battle in 1690. Today the Order sees itself as a means to defend the civil and religious liberties of Protestants and a Protestant monarchy in the United Kingdom. Annually in Northern Ireland, and some of the bordering counties of the Republic of Ireland, rural and urban areas are decorated with flags and bunting, and kerbstones painted the customary red, white and blue, in preparation for the Order, and its followers, to march through the area with their bands. For the followers of the Order this is an annual festival, part of their heritage, which they believe should be preserved and celebrated. For others it is an example of sectarianism, of Protestant triumphalism that is inappropriate for a Northern Ireland that is trying to move beyond its troubled history.

In order to make their activity more acceptable to a broader range of people, the Orange Order has in recent years begun to promote more widely the historical dimension to their activity. As a result, for the month of July, known as the 'marching season', exhibitions are mounted in Orange Halls across the province. An exhibition mounted in 2003 in a town outside Belfast celebrated 'Lisburn Orange Culture Week' (see Figs. 1.3 and 1.4). Each Orange Lodge in that District exhibited objects associated with its Lodge, such as photographs, sashes, drums and other memorabilia. Examples of banners, which had been carried on marches, were hung on the wall behind; some of the banners were still in use and others, because of their age or fragility, were now only used for display purposes. The display was impressive, the artistry on the banners illustrating the talent of the painter and telling the story of importance to the Lodge. Sometimes the banner illustrated a biblical story and at other times a moment in the history of Ireland or the Lodge. The diversity of objects exhibited ranged from the bizarre, such as knitted Orangemen toys, to ephemera, such as Lodge calendars, key rings and cups, or the everyday, such as photographs of members through the century. One member proudly displayed his collection of Orange Order badges and pins from Lodges in the Republic of Ireland and Scotland, as well as America and South Africa. This diversity in historical importance and financial value was displayed equally for visiting members.

This exhibition is a form of cultural propaganda for the Orange Order movement and this is seen in the way the history of the Order is told. The objects act as triggers to remind visitors of the richness of this form of Protestant heritage and the importance of its preservation. Although the marching season associated with the Order is linked with continued controversy and objections, no mention of this is made in the exhibitions. Instead, the displays are celebrations of the material heritage associated with the Order – many of the artefacts illustrate the skills of craftspeople. By emphasising the historical and cultural dimensions

Figure 1.3 Exhibition mounted for Lisburn Orange Culture Week, July 2003

of the Orange Order the hope is that their annual marches can be preserved as an expression of the heritage and tradition of the Orange community. The exhibitions provide a means to emphasise the longevity of the Order and the historical and cultural depth of the organisation. Furthermore, the exhibitions promote Northern Ireland as a Protestant place, loyal to the Crown and defending the interests of the Order. What struck me when I visited the exhibition was the similarity in the displays presented by the different Lodges. Again this is a useful message. This likeness forms connections between experiences and ambition. It presents unity, draws on shared understanding, and develops the idea of a common tradition. These goals are also demonstrated by the marches themselves; but the exhibitions provide a new and alternative means of promoting the idea of heritage associated with the Order. The creation and representation of a shared history through collections is a means for the groups described above to forge attachments. Community in these cases is based on a notion of

Figure 1.4 Exhibition mounted for Lisburn Orange Culture Week, July 2003

shared traditions and experiences; the collections and exhibitions are a means to develop deep attachments between members of the community.

We can turn to material culture to understand 'why some things matter'[31] and the examples provided thus far reveal that heritage matters because of what it reveals about relationships within groups and between people. The examples tell us something of the significance of objects to community groups and why the construction of collections, their display and exhibition is of value. It is important for groups to place their objects that matter on public display and this point gives us insights into the construction of community and the value of heritage. Each of these areas of concern contributes to our understanding of how communities use their material culture to construct a shared heritage, forge a group identity, define belonging to the community and build community capacities. Heritage is an active tool, and in whatever context, whether that is a national museum or a local community initiative, the heritage on display will

21

be there with purpose. Peers and Brown, in their discussion of source communities, refer to Elizabeth Edwards, who considers objects as 'sites of intersecting histories'.[32] This is a very useful idea because it illustrates that objects can become a point at which many meanings and roles are expressed – sometimes together in a productive fashion and at other times as a point of conflict where meanings are contested.

Community and museum practice

These fundamental issues of approach, impact and meaning of museums have also served to influence museum practice. The examples of community heritage projects referred to above each illustrate the relevance that heritage has for that group. They also demonstrate the importance that is placed on the preservation and display of heritage items for the construction of identity and the representation of place and as a means to bring people together as active agents. It is this awareness of value, and support from audiences, that many established museums wish to capture. As the idea of 'community' has gained relevance, questions of access, participation and representation have become regular concerns for those working in museums. This greater awareness of 'community' has had a significant impact on the museum profession and the nature of everyday museum activities such as collecting, display and the way that museums view the public. Indeed, the question of community is central to current evaluation of museums. It is increasingly being asked whether museums are serving their communities, representing their local communities within collections, and able to establish community needs. More often, it is not only the quantity of visits that is important for a museum's success; instead, there is greater interest in the diversity of visitors, the nature of the visitor experience and the impact of museums on their locality. David Dean, for instance, in one of the key texts on mounting museum exhibitions, refers to the importance of knowing your community prior to the development of an exhibition. By doing so he believes the museum can find individuals who are 'linked by common threads', which might be their culture, leisure preferences, ethnic or social affiliations or socio-economic level, and provide a ready-made audience to target.[33] Neilson, who charted the history of marketing in the Canadian museum sector, sees this greater awareness of community as a sign of 'client orientation' within the museum.[34] In his writing, interest in community is a means to increase visitor numbers. The idea of involving communities is made more subtle by the notion of 'interpretative communities', which is understood as different groups of people who might relate to museums, culture or the arts in particular ways. These too might be communities that can be identified by cultural experience, socio-economic factors or leisure practices, but considering these groups in relation to the idea of 'shared conceptual maps'[35] encourages us to take better account of the nature and causes of that diversity. The influence of the wider cultural context on the individual is well observed by Eilean Hooper-Greenhill, who promotes idea of 'interpretative communities'. She writes that although we each separately interpret our experiences, 'using our individual strategies, capabilities and preferred learning styles', our understanding is not independent from other influences. Instead, 'it is mediated, tested and developed within the context of communities of interpretation'.[36] As a result, it is not enough simply to think of the individual. In planning for museum interpretation we need to think of the social and cultural context of communities, and communities of experience, that will shape people's reactions. And rather than thinking of the audiences as a single mass, museum and exhibition planners need to develop different communicative strategies in order to appeal to the many communities that compose the whole. Similar approaches, also based on the consideration of potential audiences as communities, have also been used for greater understanding of learning in museums. This relates to what Kelly advocates as a 'communities of practice' approach to museum learning – again, identifying people with a common sense of purpose and who share expertise and passion for a subject.[37] It is important, therefore, for museums to identify learning opportunities that are of relevance to these groups and to use the skills already within the group to make best use of the museum experience.

In addition to informing museum practice, community has also become an ethical issue. As well as referring to humanity, society, ethnic and religious groups, and the public, the ICOM Code of Ethics refers to the needs of community. It states that museums should 'work in close collaboration with the communities from which their collections originate as well as those they serve'. Museums are to be in service to community, respect the interests and beliefs of communities, and create a 'favourable environment for community support'.[38] In the UK the MA Code of Ethics states that museums must now 'consult and involve communities, users and supporters' and that society can expect museums to 'seek the views of communities, users and supporters and value the contributions they make'.[39] These are institutional obligations that provide us with an indication of the responsibilities the museum profession has assumed. An ethical code uses words in a very reasoned and deliberate fashion – the public, community and society each have different meanings, and the meanings of the individual terms will shift with context. 'The public' may be a reference to people in general; 'society' may suggest an organised or structured system; and 'the community' becomes particular interest groups within that. These terms are so commonplace they frequently go undefined, but their selective use does suggest a shift in emphasis and preference. In our case, use of the term community reveals a greater interest in identifying particular groups and their interests as well as obligations to acknowledge those in museum planning.

This expectation is now central to exhibition development in the museum and, arguably, should spread to all aspects of museum work. Now it is not unusual for museums to build relationships with specific communities and use their expertise for the development of relevant exhibitions. Nightingale and Swallow, for instance, write of the success of The Arts of the Sikh Kingdoms exhibition, which opened in the Victoria and Albert Museum in London in 1999.[40] The museum holds collections of iconic material relating to Sikh culture that had been collected in the nineteenth century and has had growing contact with the Sikh community since the 1970s. Realising that access to these collections ought to be improved, and that the colonial story needed to be retold, the museum aimed to bestow cultural authority back on the Sikh community by involving them with interpretation and redisplay. In order to reach new audiences for the exhibition and education programmes, museum staff attended Sikh events, engaged Sikh leaders in an advisory role, and built a positive relationship with Sikh volunteers. Nightingale and Swallow have found that the collaboration with the Sikh community has had longer-term consequences. The museum is now considered by the Sikh community as a potential place for the construction of cultural identity. In working together, both the museum and the Sikh community had to overcome misconceptions they had of one another. And there was a concern amongst the Sikh community to use opportunities like this to overcome inequality and racial prejudice. There is also now greater expectation amongst the Sikh community that these links will be furthered. The museum is considering how to sustain this link; if Sikhs have become regular visitors to the museum; and whether the collaboration changed the 'very heart and centre' of the museum.[41]

Open Museum Glasgow

The Arts of the Sikh Kingdoms is an example of how the expertise of a specific community was used to shape exhibition planning and resulting learning programmes. It is possible to go further and to use the priority of community to rethink the entire museum concept and working practices across the institution. This is demonstrated by the example of Glasgow Museums Service, which in the early 1990s promoted the 'Open Museum' as a means to engage better with their local community. It was described as a pioneer in that field, as well as an 'iconic project'.[42] It is thought that Glasgow Museums have produced a model for how museums should engage with their communities and that this has led to a greater understanding of the processes described so far. The Director of Glasgow Museums at the time, Julian Spalding, had found that traditional approaches to attempting to build links between museums and their communities often failed. For instance, exhibitions developed by museums in community venues, or even increasing consultation with local communities, and developing projects in response, often created expectations that were difficult to sustain. Instead he recommended that local communities should be allowed to come to the museum, look at collections and borrow artefacts to create their own exhibitions in local venues – the exhibitions were not to be curator-led. The early philosophy of the museum was to 'widen ownership' by opening up the reserve collections to interested groups so as to 'create a museum . . . which is related to the lives of the people in their own communities'.[43] The approach was, and still is, one in which (as promoted on its website) 'you decide what the display is about, what goes into it, and what you want to say. And you get our support and guidance the whole way!'[44] The museum was to be an educative tool, encourage individual and group self-confidence, and become a place of empowerment. Later this philosophy was filtered through the entire Museums Service with the hope that it would 'transform the culture of museums' in the region.[45]

Evaluation of the museum, gathered through feedback from individuals who had used the facilities over a number of years, reveals the potential impact of museum projects. The study *A Catalyst for Change: The Social Impact of the Open Museum* provides accounts of those who found opportunities and activities associated with projects a positive experience. One person felt she had become more independent and confident; another referred to greater self-esteem. An oral history project is described as having made participants feel valued. A person who had experienced mental health problems found the experience of working with the Open Museum particularly profound. He spoke of feeling in the past as if he had no rights, but now 'the projects . . . have made me realise that I do have rights – I am a human being and I am allowed to express myself . . . and no-one can restrict me from doing that'.[46] The example of the Open Museum shows that active engagement with communities is a two-way process. If the goal is to open up museums, and to revisit their role, a profound rethinking of working practices needs to be undertaken. The Open Museum philosophy of making the museum stores available to community groups, so that they can use the contents for projects they have identified, shifts the authority away from the curator. The curator usually controls how collections are used, interpreted and displayed, but now the emphasis is on the user. This is not the end of the curator, or even the expert within the museum, but an example of a new approach that a museum can embrace and, given the examples cited in *A Catalyst for Change*, can do so with success. This, as many will know, is a very strategic process that must be thought out in the context of the needs of the people the museum wishes to serve and the skills and aspirations of the museum.

Rethinking museums

There are many examples of museum initiatives, like the Open Museum, which have revisited the very idea of a museum. Likewise, those contributing to museum studies have pushed the boundaries of how we think about museums and have drawn from an interdisciplinary canon to inform debate. Kyoko Murakami, for instance, writing from the point of view of psychology, and arguing the case for the creation of community museums in South African townships, discusses the idea of a museum in relation to self-awareness and consciousness. She draws on cultural psychology, which presents self-awareness and consciousness as built socially through relations with others. Community museums, Murakami states, by becoming dialogic and discursive spaces can encourage a better sense of personal and collective identity, which is vital for community regeneration. For her, the key benefit lies in revisiting the potential of museums in relation to this idea of dialogue, forming community spaces that are 'dynamic, interactive and participatory'.[47] For many who are exploring the future of museums, this idea of a museum that is more engaged is best achieved by rethinking the museum as a place that must serve society, rather than being a place that represents it. Stephen Weil considers this point as a means to update the role of museums, particularly those with a long history and established methodologies. He argues that the founding principles of these museums are no longer likely to find relevance and therefore need to be revisited. Reflecting on national museums, he describes the inheritance of what was 'a once grand and imposing structure'. 'That structure', he adds, 'with most of its ideological foundations long since rotted away, can no longer function in all of the ways in which its builders intended.' We might ask whether museum buildings and collections, founded on imperialism, social control and privilege, should be abandoned. Weil's reply is, 'few of us, though, are prepared to tear [the museum] down, or even just walk away and leave it to collapse. It still provides value and, properly adapted, it could provide far greater value still'.[48] It is this idea that museums can provide 'far greater value still' that inspires many working in the sector. Weil's proposal is not about doing away with experts in the museum or specialised collection. Rather, he is suggesting that we explore new or more appropriate reasons for having museums and their collections. It is at this point that he suggests museums should move from the position of master to being in service.

This idea of a museum 'being in service' can be approached from different perspectives. On the one hand, the issue of museums having relevance and reflecting the needs of local people may be more about institutional survival. The concern may be one of justification of a museum's existence and the collections in storage. On the other hand, the role of museums is now often being rethought in relation to notions such as equality, democracy and tolerance, which in the UK context has been described as a shift away from the 'language of paternalism' and towards 'a discourse of cultural democracy'.[49] Museums are being written about as enabling spaces which can be creative and less threatening for the visitor, and as places where 'community members can gain the skills and confidence required to take control and play an active, self determining role in their community's future'.[50] Museums are also presented as places that can stimulate interest and pride in a community's history and that can give communities the skills, experience and confidence to take control of their lives. Frequently, a museum is presented as a catalyst for developments that later become self-sustaining.[51]

These many perspectives on museums, often triggered by the introduction of the idea of community, are an indication of the importance of a more in-depth study of community and its application to museums. This book is an exploration of the numerous perspectives on the notion of community and of the profile community has in relation to interpretation, management and representation within museums. The richness of these perspectives encourages us to think more deeply about museums, their rationale and their future roles. The book draws on the museum–community relationship as a means to contribute to that discussion.

2

Understanding community

The significance of museums and heritage is continually debated, and the links made between museums and community in recent years invite us to reconsider the public role of museums, the contribution of museums to social policy, and how museums and heritage actively contribute to group identity and belonging. The concept of community is recurrent in museum policy and planning. In this context, the word 'community' is used almost indiscriminately; there is rarely qualification of what the term means and how that community is identified. Advocates promote the links between museums and community as naturally occurring, mutually beneficial, and of value to the sustainability of both. Others, however, question the reality of this idea of community and whether the goal of community could ever bring the benefits its promoters anticipate.

This chapter establishes how the term community is understood and how the notion of it has become an integral part of public life. It separates out the main uses of the idea of community and links each of these to how community is being expressed, both in the way we are beginning to understand museums and also in how we are integrating an awareness of community needs into museum development, planning and policy. To begin, the idea of community needs to be unpicked, and this must be done with an awareness of the range of uses of the term.

The literature on community, which comes mostly from the areas of social and cultural anthropology, sociology, cultural studies, development studies and public policy, can, for the purposes of this study, be broadly separated into three areas, each of which provides a key strand in this book. First is the area of community studies, which considers mainly how understanding the dynamics of community will bring a greater appreciation of the formation of identity, the creation of relationships and definitions of belonging.[1] The themes that dominate such work include how community is symbolised, the role of imagination in expressing it, and the frequently invented nature of communities. This area of community studies clearly links to writing in museum studies that has explored the meaning of objects in museums and use of display as a method to express identity, represent culture and define nations. This theme runs through the entire book. The links between museums, community and identity were discussed in Chapter 1 – the association is so pervasive you will find that such sentiment also occurs in discussions of museums and social policy, community cohesion and social capital, which are the subjects of later chapters.

A second area of community studies which is of relevance to this work is the use of community in public policy. This area focuses on how public policy has integrated the notion of community as a tool of local and national government. 'Community' is seen as a means to encourage improved hospital and medical services, more successful policing and better urban development. Within local and national government museum services, the creation of community collections, exhibitions, museums, outreach officers and education officers can be associated with this movement. For many of these examples it is important to create a public museum service that is meaningful for a broader range of people. But in some cases greater evaluation of why and how community has been incorporated needs to be undertaken before the projects can be judged a success. Often because of this lack of critique, the ease with which the word community has been slipped into so many areas of current policy and practice has come under scrutiny. Allan Cochrane, for instance, questions the integrity of the links and argues that the term has often been used as an aerosol can 'to be sprayed on to any social programme, giving it more progressive and sympathetic cachet; thus we have community policing, community care, community relations, community development, community architecture and the community programme among others'.[2] Although it is unlikely to be true of every case, Cochrane's concern is that the term is simply added on to policy, rather than integrated into the complete approach. Instead of being used as a label, Cochrane advocates that the concept becomes a means for political change and the development of more democratic processes.

This latter approach leads into the third area of community studies that is referred to in this book, which is the idea of community as a form of social action. Here one will encounter the community of resistance, and community as a form of protest and as underpinning the formation of a democracy. Community groups have used heritage and museum activity as a vehicle for protest and as integral to their social and political campaigns. Involvement of community in this context is about the creation of new 'circuits of power' and sustainable networks that promote access and inclusion and are accountable to diverse communities.[3] These are the same principles that underpin the debates in museum studies concerning social responsibilities, equality and democracy.[4]

Each of these three approaches provides a different conceptualisation of the meaning and impact of the idea of community. How this is expressed, and how each can be linked to current trends in the museum sector, provides the basis for this chapter. The first part looks at how community is symbolised and the various strands to the identification and representation of community; the second part traces the use of the idea of community in public life; and the final part considers the rise of community politics. The chapter concludes by linking each of these aspects of community to approaches to understanding the value and significance of museums.

Symbolising community

In each of the three areas of community studies identified in this chapter, the term community takes on various meanings and the community itself is recognised through different signifiers. Of the areas described above, the first is concerned with the symbolic community, the second with the civic community and the third with the political community. In each case, what is meant by the term will differ, giving rise to a multitude of versions of community and beliefs in the consequences of community development. This diversity makes the definition or recognition of community more challenging. For a moment a few words seem to clarify the idea and then, with another thought, the explanation escapes. The impossibility of settling on just one definition, that would suit many contexts, has been recognised by G.A. Hillery, who is often quoted as having identified fifty-five definitions of community used in sociological literature of the 1950s.[5] Rather than attempting to reduce this diversity to a single definition, it is more useful to consider the multitude of characteristics associated with the term. In his study of community, Gerard Delanty emphasises the range:

> Communities have been based on ethnicity, religion, class or politics; they may be large or small; 'thin' or 'thick' attachments may underlie them; they may be locally based and globally organized; affirmative or subversive in their relation to the established order; they may be traditional, modern and even post-modern; reactionary and progressive.[6]

Delanty's description is useful because it helps dispel some of the many myths associated with the term. Often community is thought to have long-established roots and to draw from traditional modes of behaviour. Many believe that the characteristics of community should be easily recognisable, such as language, race or religion. Most generally, community is thought to be associated with a fixed place. Challenging these ideas, Delanty emphasises the range of experiences of community. He argues that it is not only about the past, or nurturing communal living that is considered lost and in need of rebuilding. He also believes that community is not necessarily tied to a single place, such as a certain village or landscape; instead, it can be geographically spread but linked by an agreed interest. When community is claimed on the basis of a whole range of characteristics there is thought to be a 'thick' basis to that community. Alternatively, community may be recognised on the basis of only a few shared characteristics, in other words a 'thin' community. Delanty also makes the point that the basis of community investigation and appeal has changed. It is not principally about premodern, village or rural-based societies; instead, for many today community is about developing new power relationships and sustainability.

Although the idea of thick and thin basis to community encourages us to think about alternative means to identify community, this should not be used as a means to value those experiences or judge which community has greater depth or meaning. In rural Northern Ireland a group of women, linked only by the fact that they were all born outside the area, have come together, forming their own unique community. The group, known as Women of the World, have links with Europe, Asia, Africa and South America. The religions represented include Christian, Muslim, Hindu and Bah'ai. What unites this community is a common need for fellowship and enjoyment as well as guidance while settling in a new place. In addition the group has provided assistance for those who have experienced racism since their arrival. Supported by the Community Relations Council as well as the Northern Ireland Council for Ethnic Minorities, the group hosts events to share their cultures with the people who have lived for generations in the area. The group has also participated in local museum initiatives: they provided costume for a museum display on local identities, and workshops on aspects of their culture as part of an exhibition on cultural diversity.[7] In respect to the group as a 'community', they may be referred to as a thin community – its main connection is that of being new to the area and they don't have the thick characteristics of a long association with a single place, religion or history. Instead, recent experiences of moving to a new country, as well as a sense of difference, have brought them together. Through sharing their experiences with one another a sense of commonality has been be developed, both within the group and with those on the outside. The 'thin characteristics' that define this community are deeply meaningful and have had a significant impact on their individual and group identities – and are just as significant as numerous 'thick characteristics' of long association with place, history or religion.

This range of experiences that can be used to define a community suggests that community is a word that can roam between different contexts in an almost chameleon fashion. For some, this point would be grounds to dismiss the idea of community as outdated, vague and of little use. However, no matter how forcefully an argument of redundancy may be presented, one cannot dismiss the frequency of the use of the word and therefore its importance. As noted by Vered Amit: 'the sheer proliferation of its invocations provides a backhanded testament to the continued popular saliency of this concept'.[8]

The recent change in how community has been studied has also contributed to dispelling the many myths associated with the term. In the 1950s and 1960s community was mainly understood in functional or structuralist terms; identified as being about how groups of people are organised and interact in a given locality. In this context, community is a descriptive unit of people that emerges beyond the family and forms the basis of neighbourhood groups. Such structural analysis has more recently given way to greater consideration of the cultural, social and political dimensions of community. Consideration of how these factors aid the recognition of community and give it expression and meaning brings with it greater understanding of how community is valued and understood. For Anthony Cohen, for instance, community is formed by the attachment or commitment to a common body of symbols.[9] These symbols provide the group with meanings that are understood by the members and distinguish it in relation to others outside the community. In such cases belonging to a community is represented and strengthened by cultural markers embedded in place, history, ethnicity, sport, employment and life experiences.

To understand how community is constructed and the meanings it holds for its members it is necessary to consider how a sense of community contributes to identity formation and the creation of a sense of place, and the role of sentiment, emotion and nostalgia in the formation of group identities. Recent investigations of how groups of people have forged a sense of community reveal the complexity of the various sentiments associated with the term. Karen Evans, in her study of community and criminology, gathered information on how people in an inner city area used the term.[10] For them it was about geographical place, social networks and shared characteristics. It provided a 'motor' for collective action and was constructed symbolically. Andrew Dawson, in his investigation of responses to aging in a mining community in north-east England, shows how this community bases its feelings on the importance of the locality, the use of a language dialect that is incomprehensible to others, the emphasis on alcohol, associations with mining, and the common experiences of the aging process. These shared features, which could as easily be deconstructive, are instead valued as 'cherished mark[s] of identity'. Within this community, a conscious decision has been made to use these experiences to create unity; any variation in experience is ironed out, so as to develop a sense of sameness.[11] In the example of transnationally adopted children living in different parts of Norway, discussed by Signe Howell, community becomes an emotionally loaded place where shared experiences form the basis of a 'community of relations'. For this community, place is not significant; instead connections are made by way of shared experiences, emotions and symbols.[12] In examples of community where a sense of place is central, the disruption of place becomes a key threat and people will then pull together to construct a narrative of belonging that will counteract perceived threats.[13] Crucially, Ruud Van der Veen suggests that communities are often latent; they are 'sleeping beauties that need a kiss to be reawakened'.[14] It is what prompts this kiss that should be our concern.

These brief examples demonstrate the importance of the intangible character of community construction. Although we may think we recognise community by identifiable attributes, such as location or shared characteristics (for example, religion, sport or employment), the creation of community is bound up in the meanings associated with these symbolic markers. It is not enough to have all the characteristics of community; rather, it is essential to have the motivation to bring these together into a self-forming unit.

The community unit will not bond without reason; instead, particular circumstances must give rise for the need to come together. This point comes clear from the writing of Hugh Butcher, who has identified three main forms, which he names as the 'descriptive community', 'community as value' and 'active community'.[15] The concept of a descriptive community relates to the idea of a network of people who have something in common, either through a sense of belonging, such as a community of interest, or by identifying with certain references, like a shared territory for example. The second use of the term relates to the values associated with the concept that can be actively nurtured, such as solidarity, communal aid and connectivity. The active community relates to social initiatives that aim to develop community strengths and capacities. What is common to each of these areas is the sense of togetherness experienced by the community members, rather than isolation; their feelings of integration rather than segregation; and the promotion of inclusion within the community rather than exclusion. In each of these cases community is an active tool, an essential process that brings mutual benefits to its members. Community aids the construction of a powerful network that brings with it a sense of solidarity and purpose. This relates to what Zygmunt Bauman has identified as the most potent instigator for community: insecurity.[16] Community, he argues, is constructed when a group of people perceive an external threat; they come together as a means of self-defence. When the demand is made, external factors encourage people to identify and acknowledge characteristics that will forge community: this is demonstrated for instance when people come together to campaign against a new development or the loss of local services.

Greater consideration of the symbolism of community also helps us recognise the tensions associated with the notion. In many cases, the idea of community action and forging new relationships with communities is expressed with positive language. Zygmunt Bauman opens his study by saying that whatever community means, it is a word with a feeling; it is 'a cosy and comfortable place', where we are never strangers. For Hugh Butcher, the meaning of the word community is lost in such sentiment. He describes community is a 'hoorah word that seems to encourage warm and positive feelings at the expense of precise and meaningful analysis'.[17] Barry Schofield sees it as a term that has elusive appeal as a 'discursive resource of almost limitless potential'.[18] When further analysis is undertaken, some of the less positive associations come to light. Hand-in-hand with growing recognition of the cultural symbolism of a community is an increasing awareness of similarity and difference. As communities are established, so too is the recognition of boundaries and awareness of belonging. Emerging apparently effortlessly from shared characteristics, community is, instead, constructed in a deliberate fashion bringing security to its makers and uncertainty to those who feel they do not belong. This is achieved through the adoption of cultural codes, rituals and symbols of belonging. Critical to their success is their selectivity and ability for such symbols to be recognised by those who are not part of that community. This is important for the survival of community: it needs to be easily identified by both its members and its non-members. If community is about coming together and unity, it is equally about division and exclusion.[19]

The discussion so far highlights a central point: community is both a process and a product. It is a highly contextualised phenomenon; it can take on a whole range of characteristics according to the purpose it has been assigned. This multiplicity is at the root of why it is so difficult to assign a single definition, and is why Hillery's point, made in 1955, continues to hold true. The essential aspect of community is that the experiences within community are intangible and highly subjective. Upon this apparently insubstantial foundation, decades of public policy have drawn on the relevance of community.

Community in public life

The reasons why connections between public policy and community should have arisen are complex and draw on a number of areas, such as how community development is understood; the changing implementation of community development ideals since the popularisation of the idea in the mid-twentieth century; and the more recent approaches to community development. Consideration of this history is a means to explaining the many connections made between museum projects and community issues, which have recently become such a key area of concern for the museum sector. Engagement with this history also emphasises the importance of continual critique of the community development process and the involvement of the museum and heritage sector within it.

The rise of community in public policy

Community has been a central theme in public policy since the promotion of community development ideas in the 1950s and 1960s. At this time, focusing on community development was seen as an opportunity for the state to involve itself with civil society. This approach went on to impact on policy development locally, nationally and internationally. Looking first to global movements, government and non-governmental agencies, both national and international, continue to engage in modernisation movements in regions of the world considered less developed and in need of international aid. Since the 1950s, focus has moved from charity linked to modernisation, such as the provision of financial aid, and towards development and reform. Supporting the creation of education and health facilities would be examples of this. In comparison, community development taking place within the US, Canada and many European countries had different priorities, but within these places community development initiatives followed similar trends. Often having its roots in cooperative movements of the early twentieth century, community development in the western world, by way of societal guidance and social reform, became an essential tool of the welfare state as it emerged in the mid-twentieth century. In the 1980s, one of the aims of the politics of the 'new right', evident in both the US and the UK, was to reduce the role of the state in the marketplace and increase the primacy of the individual through a shift from 'state care' to 'community care'; and to move from a tax system concerned with welfare to one that favoured the business sector. The shift to state care involved the dismantling and privatisation of the welfare state, with greater emphasis on self-help, the voluntary sector and the community. Increasing community self-help and voluntarism was seen as a means to introduce cost savings to the public sector and to provide community development projects with greater relevancy and sustainability.[20]

The twentieth century also saw the rise of community in relation to social movements and people-centred development.[21] More radical forms of development have taken what has been termed a 'participatory approach' – one that aims to develop a greater self-awareness and confidence amongst disadvantaged people so that they can assess and take action in relation to their own living conditions, environment and other life experiences.[22] At the core of community development, as some would understand it today, are concerns such as human rights, democratic involvement and shared power, as well as providing opportunities to tackle social, economic, political and economic problems.[23] These aspects are demonstrated within the Strategic Framework for Community Development adopted in 2001 by the Community Development Xchange (CDX),[24] a UK not-for-profit organisation. The Strategic Framework lists what it regards as the core values of contemporary community development. It emphasises the importance of providing opportunities to tackle social, economic, political and economic problems as well as enhancing respect for diverse cultures. It also notes that community development is concerned with 'building active and sustainable communities', which should be 'based on social justice and mutual respect'. For them, community development is about changing power structures to remove the barriers that prevent people from participating in issues that affect their lives. Many would regard this as the new purpose of community development, although there may well be disagreements about how this would be best achieved. For some, state-led community projects that claim to have social justice or democracy as a goal may still well be aiming for this within the same old power structures. It is because of the complexity of community development, and because often the same language is used with different approaches at the core, that the interpretation of policy is sometimes difficult, and in many cases needs a longitudinal study in order to make the best assessment.

It is clear, therefore, that adopting a community approach to social, cultural and economic policy does not take a single form; instead, as shown in the review above, throughout the twentieth century involvement with community has taken different forms according to viewpoints on economic and social issues. Fraser has summarised these various approaches to community participation into four areas, which are on different points from left to right of the political spectrum.[25] The first is an approach she describes as that of anti or reluctant communitarians. For such an approach economic conservatism reigns, decision-making is top-down, and any participation is 'brief and narrowly focussed'. The second approach is that of the technical-functionalist communitarians, for whom community is managed through expert consultations with stakeholders. The third approach is that of progressive communitarians whose main goal of community work is to develop policies of empowerment that take into consideration social needs, environmental issues and social justice. The fourth approach is that of the radical/activist communitarians who adopt a transformative approach and who are interested in restructuring the global social order in a way that takes account of discrimination, oppression and environmental degradation.

This summary of community development approaches, categorised by Fraser, is useful because it demonstrates the diversity of attitudes to community and how people may use quite similar language while holding different positions. Two people may be talking about enhancing community participation, but their perceptions of its scope and the desired outcomes may be quite different. In relation to this book, when the ideas of museums, community and change are linked it will frequently be the case that there are different objectives in mind for this association. In contemporary UK policy, communitarianism is recognised as being on the rise; even so, we need to be aware that approaches within that can vary. Thinking according to these categories is also useful when considering museum projects that connect with community groups. Some will involve links with community groups, but these will be brief and adopt a largely top-down approach. In other cases community groups may be consulted as stakeholders, but again this process is managed from the perspective of the museum or heritage project. More recently museum and heritage work that supports the politics of empowerment as well as consideration of social needs has been encouraged. And finally, there are examples of museum projects that have attempted to transform museums in relation to the needs of communities.

Building community through heritage: an example from New South Wales, Australia

In Australia the Government of New South Wales has promoted the importance of being a 'community builder' and this initiative is an example of how national government, community policy and developing roles for museums and heritage have been linked. The Government has advocated stronger communities on the grounds that they encourage empowerment, inclusiveness, reconciliation, safe and healthy environments, crime prevention, and economic development and partnerships.[26] Community is regarded as the answer to social problems, as revealed by the statement made by the Premier of New South Wales in 2002 when he referred to 'community solutions' as a means to be 'tough on crime; tough on the causes of crime'.[27] The approach adopted for community was also one that was concerned with building partnerships between different tiers of governance. Community building was defined as being 'about people from the community, government and business taking the steps to find solutions to issues within their communities'.[28] This idea of using community to develop vertical attachments between people and government is an idea that has gained currency and relates to the notion of social capital, which is discussed in Chapter 4. The challenge here is to find out whether the vertical attachments are being put in place in order to naturalise government strategies through familiarisation, or whether it is a rethinking of the power relations between people and government.

This example from Australia, which demonstrates how government has been linked to community development, has also had a heritage dimension. In 2000 the Migration Heritage Centre was established in Sydney as an initiative of the Government of New South Wales in partnership with the Community Relations Commission, the Heritage Office, the Ministry for the Arts and Tourism New South Wales, and the Premier's Department. In a message on the purpose of the Centre the Premier referred to the richness of the cultural diversity of New South Wales and how the Centre was a means to 'preserve and celebrate this rich and remarkable diversity'.[29] In 2002, through its Migration Heritage Toolkit, the Centre was directly involved in the 'community building' advocated by the New South Wales Government. The purpose of the Toolkit is to encourage people in

their quality of life. Through greater empowerment the aspiration is that people and communities will be more conscious of their circumstances and the conditions that cause disempowerment. The examples of heritage projects discussed in Chapter 7 each reveal how heritage has been used as a means for empowerment. The different approaches adopted reveal the diversity of strategies that can link heritage with the goals of democracy, reflexivity and consciousness-raising. It is also the case that the very idea of empowerment has moved from the radical context into the centre stage. As a result such ideas are being raised by state politicians as well as by radical activists.

The influence of Gramsci and Freire

The conscientisation aspect of empowerment has been informed by the work of Antonio Gramsci (1891–1937) and later Paulo Freire (1921–97).[35] Both called for greater levels of community 'conscientisation', which advocated raising the self-reflective awareness of the people, rather than educating or indoctrinating them. The aim was to make people more self-aware, so that they could draw their own conclusions, rather than being informed how they should think or respond by others. This approach is linked both to Gramsci's notion of hegemony and to Freire's exploration of pedagogy, both of which have relevance for understanding museums. Gramsci, in his emphasis on hegemony, considered how a dominant group shapes society and by doing so legitimises its rule. The position of power is communicated through social institutions, such as the education or legal system, which establish 'a powerful system of fortresses and earthworks'. This system of fortresses is built into society until they are accepted as standard cultural norms, values and beliefs. Gramsci is showing that these institutions are not neutral; instead, they reinforce the existing hegemony in the interests of the most powerful social groups.[36] Furthermore, adding to the complexity of the notion, the very idea of community relies on use of the notion of hegemony. In the struggle for hegemony, a group will use economic, social and political means in the process to define itself. The past becomes a means to achieve this through the creation of 'popular memory' that will bolster the group.[37]

In his work on pedagogy Freire advocated a change in thinking concerning approaches to education and learning. His belief was that through the process of praxis the educator should enable learners to reflect on their own world. This is advanced by a change in the relationship between the educator and the learner, which should become one that encourages dialogue and reciprocal learning.[38] By this philosophy people are encouraged to have the power to assert their own voice and question dominant assumptions.[39] This has been expressed in approaches to adult education that have encouraged dialogue, enabling the oppressed to become active and reflective about their reality in order to bring about change. Mayo and Craig stress that empowerment, in this sense, is concerned with collective, community (and ultimately class) conscientisation. People, they say, are encouraged to critically assess their situations and to use what power they have to challenge the powerful, and ultimately to transform their situations through conscious political struggle.[40] It will become evident later that the processes involved in creating museum displays, and the act of public exhibition, has in some instances become a means for people to critique their own situations and feel a greater sense of empowerment.

The Gramscian notion of hegemony and the Freirean analysis of educational practice can also be used to critique the provision and work of museums. The viewpoints advocated in their work encourage greater reflection on the established practices of museums as one of the institutions that have normalised the positions of dominant social groups. Tony Bennett has already argued that a Gramscian perspective can be used to analyse the formation of museums as 'instruments of ruling class hegemony'.[41] Bennett also raises the possibility, which is important for the theme of this book, that museums are in a powerful position to attempt to reverse these political relations. He presents museums as generally thought to be 'amenable to a general form of cultural politics – one which, in criticising those hegemonic ideological articulations governing the thematics of museum displays, seeks to forge new articulations capable of organising a counter-hegemony'.[42] For this to be the case, however, Bennett recommends a better understanding of the institutional properties of the museum. The examples he discusses in *The Birth of the Museum* are the museums of the eighteenth and nineteenth centuries, which laid the foundation of museum practice in Europe and North America. In the case of the examples discussed in relation to community movements (Chapter 7), the use of museums as a form of 'counter-hegemony' is relevant because in these examples the idea of the museum is reinvented. The examples used are ones that have challenged traditional ways of exhibiting, representing histories and interpreting the past in museums. By working with the museum concept, through the formation of collections, displays and eventually museums, the community groups discussed in Chapter 7 are forging new educational relationships. It is a new form of museum that reflects the radical agendas of Gramsci and Freire, rather than a reform of the established museum.

Applying community to museum studies

This chapter has identified a threefold approach to how we should understand community and its application: community as a form of identity creation; the use of community in public life; and the political community, as demonstrated by community in social action. Importantly, we should be clear that the areas of community studies identified here all interlink, and that separating out the areas is undertaken for ease of understanding and analysis. Nevertheless, in our case, using this method to unravel how community can be approached, and applied in practice, links very well to how community has been associated with culture and the work of museums. In the UK, for instance, a recent statement on community provided by the North East Museums, Libraries and Archives Council (NEMLAC) that placed museums at the 'heart of their community' took a similar approach when describing the links between museums and community.

According to NEMLAC, museums, libraries and archives were 'contributing to community cohesion', 'reaffirming community identity' and 'responding to local circumstances and needs'.[43] Drawing from the American context, in an 'issue paper' titled *Strengthening Communities through Culture*, Elizabeth Strom, of Rutgers University, examines how culture intersects with civic life in communities.[44] Strom argues that art and culture are intrinsic to communities on all levels and suggests the main areas are: community identity; community and economic development; education and cultural literacy; and social needs. Again, these areas reflect those chiefly identified in this chapter and which form the structure of the analysis in the remainder of this book. In each case these different approaches are ways of making meaning in and with museums. It is not just the heritage or story that is being told within the museum that is relevant; it is how and why a museum is being used to communicate that message. It will emerge in later chapters that the museum is a process, a means to an end, which is constantly changed and manipulated according to the goal in mind. This is a contemporary as well as a historical phenomenon, and since we can observe it in our museums today we need to ask ourselves how we should respond. Active critique is one possibility.

3

Community development and the UK museum sector

Increasingly since the 1990s, museums are now being presented as a means to reach some of the goals of community development, such as encouraging participation of the marginalised and excluded, promotion of opportunities for self-help, and helping to bring about changes that can lead to greater social equality. The consideration of museums and heritage in relation to social improvement and change is well established and could be said to be central to the founding principles of many of our long-established local and national museums. Then the notions of change were closely associated with nineteenth-century ideas of the betterment of society. The more recent interpretation of the idea, emerging at the end of the twentieth century, has also looked to culture, museums and heritage as a means to bring about change. These new concerns, however, have more often taken on more radical agendas calling for a widespread transformation of social relations with greater access to opportunities.

The main purpose of this chapter is to show how cultural policy and community development issues have been brought close together in the UK and to emphasise the need for greater understanding of the nature and implications of this link. Not only do we need to pay closer attention to the origins of thinking about community development, but we also need to be clearer about the motivations behind its promotion. The ideals of community development are often extremely worthy and important, but when we dig deeper, and take into consideration the social and political context within which they are being developed, maybe there is greater cause for concern. It is important for us to be aware of this and to address it – if only because we want the links between museums and community change to be useful, relevant and lasting. We want the efforts of good professionals in the museum sector, who are working on various community-driven initiatives, to be successful and valued. Regular critique is part of the process of achieving this aspiration.

This chapter opens by demonstrating the currency of government-based community policy for museum planning. Following from this is an explanation of some of the key community policy approaches of the UK Government and how cultural development has been linked to these. The chapter then moves on to an explanation of how the museum sector itself has advocated the links between museums and community policy. The aspect of policy that has had greatest association with the UK museum sector is that of inclusion and this is considered in greater detail, with regard to the range of meanings associated with the idea and the issues it raises regarding the contemporary purpose of museums. The final section of this chapter invites us to participate in far greater critique of museums and community development, both as a means to understand motivations underpinning community involvement and to lead to greater recognition of the purpose and potential of museums.

New directions for the UK museum sector?

The *New Directions in Social Policy* statement issued in 2004 by the Museums, Libraries and Archives Council (MLA), the UK's national development agency for the sector, illustrates the high priority given to community development issues by the sector. In this policy-mapping document the MLA defined its priorities for the next three years, naming regeneration and sustainable communities, social inclusion, neighbourhood renewal and community agendas as key themes.[1] The MLA argued in *New Directions in Social Policy* that the priorities it emphasised were developed in response to a general acceptance that museums and galleries must address national policy issues. Shortly after the publication of *New Directions in Social Policy*, the MLA brought its key priorities to national attention by placing them in a bulletin produced for the Delivering Sustainable Communities Summit. The Summit, held in Manchester in early 2005, involved 2000 delegates and was hosted by the Deputy Prime Minister and supported by senior cabinet members from across Government. The main concern of this meeting was to demonstrate Government commitment to the creation of sustainable communities and to foster agreement amongst the delegates on the means to achieve this. The MLA's participation in the Summit reveals their commitment to national policy and the value they place on forging awareness amongst those outside the sector of the relevance of museums to wider issues. Table 3.1 summarises the contents of the MLA

Table 3.1 MLA bulletin for the Sustainable Communities Summit (2005): how museums can contribute to sustainable communities

Key contributions	Examples provided
Fostering and creating pride in communities	Museums as part of area regeneration
Celebrating local identity and sense of place	Community archive project
Providing safe and trusted public spaces	Working with refugee communities
Promoting vibrant local cultures	Creativity workshops in museums and libraries
Empowering and engaging people from all backgrounds	Life-long learning projects
Creating cohesive communities	Museums as community hubs
Providing access to other services	Integrating with other public services

bulletin produced for the Summit and it demonstrates the new language of museum development. In the bulletin the MLA argued that museums are core institutions for delivering sustainable communities, emphasising that 'communities need museums, libraries and archives' and that museums 'lie at the very heart of communities'. The MLA bulletin also gives priority to the notion of social capital, described as 'the glue that binds communities together', and culture is presented as playing 'a major role in determining how much social capital exists within a community'.[2] The MLA is here establishing museums as central to the formation of community and to the creation of community identity. It is suggesting that communities need museums to recognise themselves, and that museums are essential to the formation and survival of community.

The *New Directions in Social Policy* document is a clear example of how planning for museums, libraries and archives in the UK is fully integrated into national strategies on social issues. The MLA document reveals new alliances; it shows that the MLA is sympathetic to embracing Government policy and building it into their forward planning. The MLA statement reports on the importance of recent UK Government policies for shaping the future of museums. For instance, the five-year plan issued by the Office of the Deputy Prime Minister in 2005, *Sustainable Communities: People, Places and Prosperity*, is described as 'especially relevant to the MLA sector'.[3] In addition, the work of the Home Office in relation to communities, active communities, race, cohesion, equality and faith as well as 'crime and offender management' is noted as significant for museum planning.[4] It has long been acknowledged that museums are not isolated institutions; instead, it is accepted that museums reflect the social and political contexts in which they exist. This example, relating to community development, reveals that UK museum policy is very clearly determined by the concerns of central government.

For the museum sector the importance of *New Directions in Social Policy* is threefold. In the first place it is placing the sector as concerned with contemporary issues. Museums are not to be seen as the distant houses of history, art, archaeology or geology, which has been the perception of them in the past. Instead, museums are being presented as places that can use display as a means to explore relevant issues. Secondly, not only is the document evidence that the museum sector is prepared to embrace these new concerns, those leading the sector are attempting to place museums at the cutting edge of new thinking about those issues. The very idea and practice of community development has been much debated and new methods are emerging. Key policy makers in the museum sector are welcoming the changing views on how to approach social problems and are placing museums as ideal to forward these new methodologies. Finally, museums are presenting themselves as places that can have an impact on the breadth of social problems. Rather than only locating themselves as places that can contribute to the alleviation of one or another social problem, the museum sector is instead being presented as ideally placed to explore the shared and linked characteristics of a number of problems. Therefore, it is not unusual to find museums frequently presented as places that have much to offer in relation to the combined problems of community cohesion, sustainability, inclusion and regeneration.

Indeed it has now come to the point at which the museum sector is not just advocating the very idea of linking museums to community development agendas. Instead, some in the UK museum sector are confident about the positive contributions they have already made to these social policy areas and they are keen to celebrate the contribution museums have made to society. One such body is that made up of the Directors of UK National Museums and Galleries (NMDC), which, through its publication *Museums and Galleries: Creative Engagement* published in 2004, confidently described the impact of museums in various social policy areas.[5] According to the National Museum Directors' Conference (NMDC), the museums and galleries sector has gone through a 'sea-change' and has adopted a proactive approach to its role in society.[6] *Creative Engagement* identifies numerous projects that are examples of innovative practice in museums, which are outside the usual view of what museums and galleries do. A project run by the National Museums of Scotland, for instance, involving socially excluded young people is cited as a good example of community engagement. This project used a visual arts and performance-based company to help study objects in a new and creative way.[7] Another example is that of the National Museum of Photography, Film and Television in Bradford, which is praised for working with Asian youths who had been using the museum as a 'hanging-out' space. Some museum staff felt that the youths could become a threat to collections, and through workshops designed specifically for this group the relationship between the museum and young people improved. Later the museum adopted their workshops to form part of a surveillance programme for those who had been arrested, and later released, for their involvement in local riots. The NMDC account of the project concludes by stating that not only have networks between various agencies in Bradford been improved, but vandalism in the museum has reduced by 70 per cent and two of the former 'troublemakers' have gone on to work in the museum as youth mentors.[8]

Creative Engagement provides accounts of twenty-seven examples of how museums in the UK have taken a proactive approach to working with local communities and how these new links have benefited both the museum and society. For NMDC these accounts are examples of how the museum profile is changing from 'inward-looking institutions to significant agents of change at both the individual and community level'.[9] NMDC describe museums as places that 'create social capital, educating and empowering individuals and groups alike, creating networks and stimulating dialogue'.[10] The numerous projects described outline how museums have made connections with young people, have initiated public debate on controversial issues and have transformed their collections through new partnerships. It is descriptions such as these that provide the evidence for the threefold approach to how museums are now engaging with community development issues, as described above in relation to the *New Directions* statement. The case studies in the NMDC document are not only used as evidence that museums can explore relevant issues; they are also used as examples of how museums can place themselves at the cutting edge of the means to solve social problems, and as proof that museums are a possible venue where the shared characteristics of numerous social concerns can be tackled. It is important for us to explore the origins of these beliefs and to find out how they 'crept up' on the museum sector. Only then can we analyse the usefulness of this new approach.

Community in UK public policy

During the 1990s community development was increasingly placed at the heart of UK Government policy. Government policy and guidance notes have made repeated reference to the value of community cohesion, community regeneration and the establishment of sustainable communities, as well as notions such as the 'active' community, the 'healthy' community, the 'creative' community and the 'confident' community. These different examples of terminology, which suggest some subtle differences, are linked by an agreement on the value of focusing on the community as a building block of society and as a means to achieve the aims of Government. Each of these examples of Government-led community development differs in emphasis. In brief, the concern of community cohesion is the creation of bonds; the aspiration of community regeneration includes lower unemployment and better housing; and the sustainable community relates to the maintenance of these improvements. Despite these differences in outcomes, the ideas relate to each other and are interlinked and interdependent. According to the rationale of such documents, a cohesive community will aid regeneration and, once community bonds have been formed, the community is likely to become more sustainable. Likewise, a community that is active, healthy and creative will tend to be more confident. The Government reports that have promoted the ideas of cohesive, confident and sustainable communities provide us with some access to how 'community' is being conceptualised and employed. The reports also reveal the context within which museum-based community initiatives have been and continue to be developed.

The community development areas named by the Museums, Libraries and Archives Council as of relevance to the UK museum sector are numerous and overlapping. The four policy areas named in *New Directions in Social Policy*, sustainable communities, social inclusion, neighbourhood renewal, and community agendas, are interrelated: the experience of one will affect the other. What is thought to link these four areas is the experience of community cohesion. This has become something that Government strives for as an ideal, the lack of cohesion often being considered to be at the root of social and economic problems. Cohesion, conveyed as the touchstone at the heart of community, suggests a cooperative and peaceful society. It is because community cohesion is thought to be lacking that many Governments have placed it high on the public agenda.

Cohesion and culture

Community cohesion can be investigated in numerous ways but it is generally accepted that it relates to the psychological sense of community and is based on the sense of belonging, the nature of social support, group solidarity, rootedness and social ties.[11] These notions are reflected in how the UK Government understands community cohesion, as demonstrated by the definitions provided by the Community Cohesion Unit within the Home Office (see Table 3.2).[12]

The key buzzwords of community cohesion, such as belonging, valuing diversity and citizenship, have found resonance in the UK cultural sector. The case to draw the Government agenda of community cohesion into the cultural sector has been made in various reports published in the last five years. *Building Cohesive Communities*, published in December 2001, established the UK Government's commitment to civil renewal as a response to 'deep fracturing of communities on racial, generational and religious lines'. To reverse this trend the Government recommended the improvement of housing, the development of employment opportunities, and enhancing the role of education. It advocated the promotion of dialogue and understanding between communities and the building of community through debating identity, values and citizenship. This is thought to contribute to the cohesive community, which is identified as one in which people are united 'around a common sense of belonging regardless of race, culture or faith'.[13] In this report the Government proposed a multilayered approach to resolving these problems. The Government also emphasised the importance of strengthening community leadership, responding better to the needs of young people, and harnessing the potential of sport and culture. Sport and culture are presented as a means of 're-engaging disaffected sections of the community, building shared social capital and grass roots leadership through improved cross-cultural interaction'.[14] The *Building Cohesive Communities* report specifically refers to the learning potential of museums as places where cross-cultural themes could be explored.

Culture is now firmly established in the UK as a means to foster community cohesion. This is clearly demonstrated in *Bringing Communities Together*

Table 3.2 Community cohesion as defined by the UK Home Office (2005)

Community cohesion was seen as crucial to promoting greater knowledge, respect and contact between various cultures, and to establish a greater sense of citizenship.

A cohesive community is one where:

- there is a common vision and a sense of belonging for all communities;
- the diversity of people's different backgrounds and circumstances is appreciated and positively valued;
- those from different backgrounds have similar life opportunities; and,
- strong and positive relationships are being developed between people from different backgrounds in the workplace, in schools and within neighbourhoods.

through Sport and Culture, the record of a seminar held in Oldham in March 2004 and later published by the Department of Culture, Media and Sport.[15] The seminar brought practitioners together to share experiences of how sport and culture had been used to build community cohesion in their areas of England. In the Foreword to *Bringing Communities Together* Tessa Jowell, then Minister for Culture, Media and Sport, described sport and culture as 'powerful tools for building community cohesion', as 'natural opportunities' for people to come together, and as a means to create 'local pride and belonging'.[16] As well as recounting the successes of various projects across the north of England, the participants noted the elements of best practice that were vital to successful engagement with local communities. Four central themes were identified as essential for effective community projects: needs analysis, partnership working, growing and adapting, and, finally, evidence and evaluation. The seminar also suggested a fifth – celebration – the feeling that gives 'a sense of pride, place and belonging'. These five elements are identified as crucial to the sustainability of projects and to the cohesive community.

Central Government policy is also shaping local management. *Community Cohesion – An Action Guide*, produced by the Local Government Association in 2004, defines community cohesion as based upon the local experience and as at the core of forming a secure society:

> Community cohesion lies at the heart of what makes a safe and strong community. It must be delivered locally through creating strong community networks, based on principles of trust and respect for local diversity, and nurturing a sense of belonging and confidence in local people. Effectively delivering community cohesion also tackles the fractures in society which may lead to conflict and ensures that the gains which changing communities bring are a source of strength to local areas.[17]

The communities that are being targeted by this policy are those of 'different faiths and beliefs',[18] as well as vulnerable groups such as people in care, youth groups, older adults and traditionally excluded groups. The many examples of projects undertaken around Britain to promote community cohesion, which are described in the action guide, reveal that the approach is one of local government working with communities at risk to address issues of citizenship, belonging and pride. Different examples presented in the report illustrate how consultation between local government and community groups has led to the drawing up of a common set of values regarding quality of life aspirations, the development of community cohesion charters, and the production of community cohesion delivery plans.

Stories in a Suitcase, Kirklees

Arts, sports and cultural services are advocated by *Community Cohesion* as 'powerful tool to engage all sections of the community and break down barriers between them' and as 'an opportunity for "joined up working" with other public and voluntary agencies'.[19] Examples are given that show how people in urban and rural areas have used arts and culture in order to raise perceptions of co-hesion. Liverpool City Council attempted to engage previously 'unheard voices' in cultural programmes. A visual and performing arts scheme in Lancashire is described as bringing together a culturally diverse community. In Gateshead communities have been united through music, and an oral history exhibition in Kirklees was described as enhancing community cohesion by celebrating the multicultural history of the area.[20] Each of these initiatives is cited as an example of best practice. Furthermore, they are named as initiatives that should be used to inspire similar enterprises elsewhere in the country.

The Kirklees exhibition, titled 'Stories in a Suitcase', opened in a local com-munity hall in May 2002 and was later published in a book of the same title by the Kirklees Metropolitan Council.[21] Developed by the Community History Service of Kirklees Metropolitan Council, the exhibition originated from an approach by a group of local people who wanted to celebrate the history of their area. Based mainly on interviews with local residents, and illustrated by personal photographs and family documents, the exhibition shared the experience of all being 'comers-in' as the common link between people. The exhibition was hosted, for just over two months, in a local community centre. In this space suitcases were displayed, each containing the story of different incomers to the area. Panels along the walls described further histories and experiences. In the publication that came after the exhibition, the Centre Manager, Abdul Aslam, described both his uncertainty at the beginning of the project and its success when it was finally realised. Aslam referred to the negative perceptions people had of the area and believes that the event helped to change people's thinking. For him it was a 'wonderful project that brought different families and groups of people in Ravensthorpe together, enabling them to share each other's stories, values and traditions'.[22]

For the Community Education Officer, who guided the development of the exhibition, it was regarded as an opportunity to 'develop a fresh sense of identity and pride in the town and to encourage groups and individuals to learn about each other and get involved in community action'.[23] Over forty families contri-buted oral histories to the project, sixteen people contributed life stories to the exhibition, and young people from a local school contributed their 'visionary valises' depicting their vision of the future of the area and their place in it. The opening of the exhibition was described as a 'celebration' attended by over 200 people and included games and music. Acknowledged by the then Home Secretary as 'a shining example of promoting "community cohesion"', reflection on the initiative by the Community Education Officer provides a hint of the social impact of the project. Her description of the project evokes a sense of it improving vertical links between different levels of government as well as horizontal links between groups of people:

> We cannot claim that this project has solved Ravensthorpe's difficulties regarding drug abuse, crime and racism. We can, however, say that the success and accessibility of the exhibition and book has enabled disparate groups to come together to celebrate positive aspects of their history, their

present identity and their future. These groups are being encouraged to continue their alliance, in partnership with Kirklees Services like our own, to address local issues with optimism, tolerance and increased understanding.[24]

The project was supported by the Dewsbury West Neighbourhood Management Pathfinder (DWNMP), a scheme funded by the Neighbourhood Renewal Unit of the Office of the Deputy Prime Minister. Established in 2002, DWNMP aims to deliver improved levels of community cohesion, better housing and environment, better health and education, and lower levels of crime and unemployment. The Stories in a Suitcase exhibition was described by the Neighbourhood Manager as contributing to the neighbourhood community cohesion strategy by 'working towards a more integrated community'.[25] Since the publication of the *Community Cohesion* guide in 2003, and the Stories in a Suitcase book in 2004, the Kirklees exhibition is used as evidence of the positive impact of the Home Office on crime reduction, antisocial behaviour, and policing the creation of active communities. In a written answer submitted to the House of Commons in March 2005, the Community Cohesion Pathfinder Programme at Kirklees is described as contributing to building 'strong, active and harmonious communities'; the Stories in the Suitcase exhibition was as 'popular with both white and Asian residents living in Kirklees and helped change local perceptions about the differences between community groups'.[26]

This scheme and the connections it makes between different levels of government is an example of how the various initiatives become interlinked and how national policy trickles down to impact on a local level. The idea for the exhibition came from local people, and then it was integrated into the established cohesion agenda and fed back into the system as an example of success.

The dominance of community policy

Whether the Government strategy is one of a cohesive, active community or sustainable community, we cannot escape the fact that 'community' is at the core. It is common for all these community strategies to reoccur within cultural policy and to shape planning for the future of museums, archives, libraries and the arts. This is demonstrated in the document *Sustainable Communities: People, Places and Prosperity*, a five-year plan published in 2005 by the Office of the Deputy Prime Minister. Its objective is the creation of sustainable communities, presented as places where people will want to live. The sustainable community will be active, inclusive and safe. There will be high levels of participation, a high-quality built and natural environment, good transport, and a diverse local economy. In addition there will be 'a strong local culture', 'shared community activities' and 'well-kept parks'. It is believed that the sustainable community will lead to decreased homelessness, improved health and transport, enhanced economic development, and better conditions for education and learning.[27] Within this report, activity that has used culture as 'a stepping stone to wider urban generation' is promoted;[28] and culture is presented as having 'a central role in bringing people together and building a sense of community, and in breaking down barriers'.[29] Cultural activity is only one of many activities promoted as necessary for the formation of the sustainable community; enhancing local economies, skills, transport and infrastructure are also promoted as crucial. Nevertheless, culture is there, amongst these more traditional tools of community development, as a means to contribute to community change.

Further suggestions about the context within which community policy is being developed by the UK Government is provided by the Home Office report *Confident Communities in a Secure Britain: The Home Office Strategic Plan 2004–8*, published in 2004. This report opens with a Foreword from Prime Minister Tony Blair that describes the 'grim legacy' inherited from the previous Government. He writes that under their administration crime had doubled, vulnerable people felt like prisoners in their homes, and 'decent families and communities were close to giving up the struggle against thugs'.[30] To reverse this situation the Government's approach is to develop a sense of 'citizenship, identity and cohesion', which would be achieved by having a tough stance on crime, enforcement and public protection. They also hope this will be achieved by enhancing the security of borders and investment in 'active citizenship, the strength of our communities and the voluntary sector'.[31] These words from the Prime Minister and also his Home Secretary suggest a menacing and threatening society within which a return to the active and participatory community will be the redeemer. Here the Government is responding in the way Zygmunt Bauman identified – calling on community at a time of insecurity. Museums have been drawn into this approach; in a number of Government documents, which will be referred to later, museums, the arts and culture are suggested as a means to form this participatory community and raise the level of cohesiveness.

In this latest example of how community is understood, and employed, the Home Office is attempting to encourage people to become more involved. The idea is for communities to take responsibility by becoming more self-aware and developing their capabilities. *Confident Communities* is promoting a concept of community that is concerned with enhancing a sense of ownership and accountability. In this example the proposed outcome of community is good governance. By improving vertical bonds between Government and the people it is thought that state priorities and policies will have a greater chance of success. This is further emphasised in the Community Development section of the Home Office Civic Renewal Unit, which defines its main task as being to 'increase people's active involvement in the governance of their communities'. The Home Office provides a number of ideas of how this could be achieved. They present the idea of community capacity building, which refers to the enhanced possibilities brought to people by belonging to a group. In addition, the Home Office plans to encourage people to become more engaged by the formation of partnerships between the community and the voluntary sector. The Home Office also hopes that the community agenda will lead to civil reform, indicated by a more peaceful and better-operating society.[32] The entire message is one of integration and assimilation – it is the renewal of community according to the objectives of Government.

Bringing the Government agenda to the cultural sector

In the UK the Department of Culture, Media and Sport (DCMS) is responsible for bringing the priorities and policies of Government to the cultural sector and ensuring the efficiency of its sponsored bodies, such as museums and galleries, the historic environment and the arts.[33] The current strategic objectives of DCMS, which are communities, children and young people, and the economy, reflect Government priorities, and in this DCMS is an additional means of dissemination.[34] *Culture at the Heart of Regeneration*, published in 2004 by DCMS, demonstrates well the links between Government strategy and planning for the cultural sector.[35] This report sets the scene for how the arts, culture and sport can contribute to community regeneration. Culture is named as 'driving' regeneration; it is a 'catalyst', and a means for 'organic development'.[36] These buzzwords are used to convey a methodology of development which has culture at its core. This methodology is described as one that includes community consultation and participation, revitalisation of the historic environment, the development of mixed-use projects with local public services, and using solutions that have emerged from the communities. The DCMS states that its approach to nurturing the links between culture and regeneration is one that involves building partnerships between government and the private and voluntary sectors; spreading good practice on linking culture and regeneration; and, strengthening the evidence base on the impact culture has on regeneration.[37] Examples such as the formation of iconic buildings, the enhancement of creative industries, and the establishment of heritage areas are all cited as contributing to local regeneration. The opening of Tate Modern in London and the visual and performing arts centre The Lowry in Greater Manchester, are both cited as having brought high quantities of public and private investment to their local areas.[38] *Culture at the Heart of Regeneration* is an example of an approach that presents culture as a vehicle to achieve urban and rural regeneration. It is not enough to aim for improved housing and transport; instead, recognised and valued cultural opportunities and spaces are advocated as a means to improve the local quality of life and attract tourism and investment.

The UK publications referred to so far provide a view of the character of the nation at the beginning of the twenty-first century. They are a record of the social and political views of New Labour and an interpretation of the role the state should play in society. Their various policy documents also reveal the contemporary approach to community development. As discussed in the previous chapter, this is one that is presented as people-centred and is related to the rise of the politics of the left. Under New Labour in the 1990s there was a move away from the top-down approach of the previous administration and towards increased levels of community involvement. More radical forms of development have taken what has been termed a 'participatory approach' – one that aims to develop a greater self-awareness and confidence amongst disadvantaged people in the hope that they will become more prepared to assess and take action in relation to their own living conditions, environment and other life experiences.[39] This approach has also had an impact on cultural policy and practice. Guided by national policy, which has encouraged a general shift in thinking, museum policy strategists are now engaging more fully with the broader language of community development. The interest in access and social inclusion, which was demonstrated in museum policy and planning documents in the mid-1990s, has now widened to include other concerns. Museum policy is now also referring to ideas such as empowerment, cohesion and participation. It is now necessary for those engaged in shaping the museums of the future to be confident in addressing these additional community development concepts.

The background to museums embracing social policy

Recent community development policy in the UK has embraced myriad policies that relate to what central Government has recognised as 'problems within society'. In each case the museum and cultural sectors have responded, placing these new concerns at the core of debate amongst their peers. This section will navigate you through those responses and debates to expose the origins and emphasis of the new directions the sector is moving in.

The Comedia report *Use or Ornament? The Social Impact of Participation in the Arts*, published in 1997, was perhaps the first major contribution to a new understanding of how museums could involve themselves with contemporary ideas of community development and social policy.[40] Comedia, a UK-based research group that concerns itself with understanding the role of creativity in improving the vitality of cities, drew on case study research to develop a better understanding of how participation in the arts brings social benefits. The approach taken began with the belief that although the impact of participation in the arts can often be quantified (for instance through economic returns), the more important benefits have an intangible quality. So instead of looking to clear evidence of the impact of museums or heritage on income generation in the local economy, it was considered more representative to look also at the 'softer benefits', such as those from meeting new people. Drawing on an evidence-base of experiences in the UK, the US and Finland, *Use or Ornament?* cited many examples of the positive impact of participation in the arts. The report emphasised, for instance, the returns from personal development, the greater community links, and the empowerment of groups of people through participation in the arts. The positive returns from improvement of local image and identity, higher levels of creativity and the benefits of sheer enjoyment were also highlighted. The enhancement of local identity was considered in relation to developing greater pride in local traditions and cultures that brings people together and transforms people's perceptions of an area. Examples of community theatre, an art project and a community archive are outlined as the means by which this has been achieved. How these benefits contributed to greater sense of belonging, pride in the local area and enhanced community capacity was also considered. Case studies provided evidence that participation in the arts reduced feelings of isolation, helped develop contacts, and brought about greater under-standing between and within communities. The wealth of examples provided in *Use or Ornament?*, and how they were analysed, usefully documents the potential of the arts. For many who have successfully participated in cultural programmes these benefits will come as no surprise. The key for the cultural sector however, is, to share and spread these outcomes amongst those who don't usually participate and to ensure that these associations do lead to the creation of positive relationships or experiences.

These benefits, discussed in *Use or Ornament?*, can be directly related to the measures of deprivation used as an indication of the need for community develop-ment. In the UK a 'Deprivation Index' is calculated according to a matrix of seven factors, such as income and crime, which combine to give a general sense of the wellbeing of an area.[41] It is a hard measure of social need and is often used by a range of government departments to target social policy and investment geographically. Changes in these indices have become central to planning com-munity development policy and measuring its impact. It should be remembered that the indices are not necessarily a value-free indication of deprivation. Instead, periodically revisited and recalculated, each version differs in the weighting given to particular factors and therefore provides a different perception of relative deprivation. According to the changing calculations, areas may be presented as relatively better or worse off than before.[42] The impact of participation in the arts, as described in *Use or Ornament?*, can be considered in relation to the indices of the Deprivation Index. Through a rise in self-confidence people became more willing to take up education and training opportunities, which could potentially lead to employment and higher income levels. Enhanced creativity and opportunities for enjoyment were shown to have a positive impact on health and well-being. In addition, higher levels of empowerment allowed people to make greater use of services available to them, and greater levels of social cohesion were shown to have led to a reduction in crime.

Since the publication of *Use or Ornament?* in 1997 the evidence base of the benefits of participation has continued to grow and there has been greater local and central government support for using arts, heritage and culture for social purposes. In addition, there has been a general acceptance that not only the various social issues that can be identified are interrelated; the solutions identi-fied to tackle them must also be brought together. Therefore, although we can identify policy documents that may focus particularly on social inclusion, and others that seem to make community cohesion or participation their main focus, it is true that these documents overlap and the recommendations of one will influence the other. For the museum sector this means that we cannot just focus on one social policy area; instead, the sector really needs to be familiar with the approaches and methodologies of a whole host of concerns. This broadening of interest, which was also recognised by the *New Directions in Social Policy* document referred to at the beginning of this chapter, brings additional challenges. For a start, those who are new to Government policy on social and community issues are likely to find that it is highly jargonistic,[43] with language that could well be alienating. Little explanation of terminology is provided and the distinctions between one social policy area and another are often left unexplored.

Although it is satisfying to go through the literature to reveal the differences in political and social attitudes revealed by different times, methods or approaches to social policy or community development, this is a luxury many working in the museum sector would not have. In addition, different government departments and their responsibilities can be difficult to distinguish; for instance, it is often not clear why different departments seem to be issuing policies in similar areas, what the relationship between these departments might be, and whether one has a lead role over the other. As a final point, when reviewing government policy in community development, frequently the move between policies and priorities, from one period to another and between departments, is undertaken with little explanation or advice. This practice is in itself exclusionary and is bound to lead to policy fatigue, lack of interest and possibly even scepticism amongst those who are expected to take on these recommendations. Some relief is found for those in the museum sector by organisations, such as the Museums Association and the Museums, Libraries and Archives Council, who provide briefing articles on key areas of social policy, and related reports. Together these publications provide a route into the policy area. However, there is still a need for a longitudinal study that will provide far greater scrutiny and informed critique.

The museum sector and social inclusion

One area that has been subject to scrutiny is social inclusion and how it has been linked with museums. UK Government policy on social inclusion in the 1990s laid the foundation for more recent policy concerning cohesion, participation, regeneration and, currently, the development of social capital. Museum policy in the UK has responded to the social inclusion challenge and is now incorporating these further policy considerations into planning. As we step through the maze of community policy it is possible to distinguish a trend and identify the evolving acceptance and emphasis placed on the contribution of museums and culture to social policy. The most dominant policy issue is that of social inclusion, which has since evolved into statements on museums in relation to cohesion, participation and regeneration. Social inclusion was a key area of debate for the museum sector in the mid-1990s – it dominated museum conferences,[44] research projects[45] and strategic planning in museums.[46] Inclusion was welcomed by many, who saw it as the means to refocus museums, bring new relevance to collections and open the doors to new and important audiences. For some, the idea of social inclusion was unwelcome. Those critics argued that it drew people away from the true purposes of museums, such as the development and preservation of collections, and introduced museums to political pandering in an area where they are not best placed to contribute.[47] The headline-grabbing debate regarding the wisdom of bringing the social inclusion agenda into museums has not gone away; instead, it seems to have calmed with time. As this has happened the social policy agenda within museums has become an established, and more generally accepted, part of museum work.

The publication in 1998, by the Social Exclusion Unit, of the report *Bringing Britain Together: A National Strategy for Neighbourhood Renewal* was, arguably, the trigger for the change in how culture, arts and museums have been viewed in relation to contemporary social policy. The focus of this report was regeneration, and in contemporary UK policy regeneration is defined as 'the positive transformation of a place – whether residential, commercial or open space – that has previously displayed symptoms of physical, social and/or economic decline'.[48] Recent regeneration policies have looked to initiatives that will tackle these various symptoms together. Policies are looking to impact jointly on the alleviation of poor housing, high crime and unemployment as well as issues such as community breakdown. *Bringing Britain Together* outlined the Social Exclusion Unit's commitment to investment in people, the involvement of communities and the development of what it described as 'integrated approaches'.[49] The report's remit was to develop 'integrated and sustainable approaches' to solving the problems of crime, drugs, unemployment, community breakdown and poor education in deprived areas.[50]

The language used in this new national strategy was that which promoted investment in people and involvement of communities. The policy approach was to be one of integration and long-term commitment, with a positive impact on the poorest neighbourhoods as the main goal. Solving the problems of social exclusion was presented as central to neighbourhood renewal. Defined as 'what can happen when people or areas suffer from a combination of linked problems such as unemployment, poor skills, low incomes, poor housing, high crime environments, bad health, poverty and family breakdown',[51] inclusion strategies have since become core work of many government departments. The main means for the Government to forward this new agenda was through the New Deal for Communities initiative. By placing community at the 'heart' of partnerships, planning and implementation, New Deal was established with the aim to tackle multiple deprivations.[52] Since their inception in 1998, the Government estimates that £39 billion has been invested in partnerships that relate to key themes such as poor job prospects, high levels of crime, educational underachievement, poor health, housing and physical environment. In an evaluation of the initiative during 2001–5, around 7 per cent of the NDC Delivery Plans relating to community development were classified as an arts or culture project.[53]

With the Social Exclusion Unit established, *Bringing Britain Together* set the priorities for Government action. The first stage in this process was the formation of eighteen Policy Action Teams (PATs). Each PAT was to investigate and recommend in areas ranging from 'jobs' and 'skills' to 'unpopular housing' and 'information technology'. Policy Action Team 10 (PAT 10), led by the Department of Culture, Media and Sport, was established specifically to address the role of arts and sport. Its goals were clear: to 'draw up an action plan with targets to maximise the impact of arts, sport and leisure policies in contributing to neighbourhood regeneration and increasing local participation'; and to 'maximise the impact on poor neighbourhoods of Government spending and policies on arts, sport and leisure'.[54] To some extent, the description of PAT 10 also suggests a lack of depth in knowledge and understanding of the link that can be made between the arts and social change. The authors admitted their amazement with the comment 'the arts have sometimes played a surprisingly important role in turning around poor neighbourhoods'. Despite this, they go on to ask a lot of the sector. A few sentences later they declare: 'involving the whole community in a major arts or sport project can build networks and open doors to other community activities'. According to them, it can also 'turn around a neighbourhood's image of itself and combat a negative reputation, tackle youth disaffection and help to build links between different ethnic communities in a neighbourhood'.[55] This leap, from astonishment at the link to arts as the panacea, suggests a simplification of the potential relationship. Such easy declarations are rarely convincing and often disconcerting. This over-generalisation regarding the cure-all approach to museums and community problems is also a key reason why many within the sector have spoken out against the association. Adding to this, these recommendations often were not followed by practical action. As identified by Newman and McLean, the PAT 10 announcement brought little extra funding to the sector,[56] which suggests that the potential was not fully accepted. For now, however, we must take the *Bringing Britain Together* report as the prompt that it was. It was the beginning of a period during which policies that involved arts and museums with social inclusion, regeneration and sustainability programmes were the norm. We entered a time when inclusion was the buzzword in the sector and it dominated museum debate.

The resulting report of Policy Action Team 10, published by DCMS two years later, focused on the goal to provide an action plan with targets to maximise the impact of arts, sports and leisure policies in contributing to neighbourhood regeneration and increasing local participation. The Foreword from Chris Smith, then Secretary of State for Culture, Media and Sport, opens with the line that the report is a consideration of how to 'maximise the impact on poor neighbourhoods of Government spending and policies'. It is clear from this statement that the concern is, first and foremost, Government and increasing the impact of Government. Culture, arts and leisure are being used as a communication medium to pass on Government priorities. Unsurprisingly, this is the objective of the Minister for Culture, Media and Sport and the Department.

Later reports continued to forward the idea that arts and culture can make an important contribution to local regeneration and development. The Department of Culture, Media and Sport's draft policy report *Centres for Social Change: Museums Galleries and Libraries for All* (2000)[57] and the final report *Libraries, Museums, Galleries and Archives for All* (2001),[58] published eight months later, established how the Government proposed to implement the recommendations of PAT10. It outlined the Government vision for how museums, and related sectors, should extend their services to explore and implement procedures to tackle social exclusion. The recommendation to place inclusion at the core of museum planning was demonstrated in the 2001 DCMS report. DCMS suggested that the museum sector should undertake research and promote activities to combat social exclusion; that museums should receive guidance on setting objectives and evaluating outcomes of activities designed to tackle social exclusion; and that social exclusion strategies should be included in developing standards and accessing funding and support for the museum sector.[59]

The DCMS report triggered a threefold response from the museum sector. The first, and the most significant, was the widespread adoption of inclusion strategies into strategic planning for the sector. Secondly, the period immediately after the publication of the report saw enhanced investment in research that provided an evidence base for the role of museums and how inclusion work should be undertaken.[60] Thirdly, there are examples of the museum sector responding with examples of inclusion work that was already central to work practice in the sector. The report *Museums and Social Exclusion* published by the Group for Large and Local Authority Museums (GLLAM), for instance, mapped the level of activity and commitment to social inclusion work amongst its membership and provided an account of past projects that contributed to this area. Museums were cited as referring to social inclusion work as 'fundamental to our existence', 'a key element in our service planning' and 'increasingly important'.[61] The projects undertaken are described as 'inspirational, creative' and 'demonstrably life-enhancing for those involved'.[62] Feedback from individual projects across the GLLAM members describes how involvement in museum projects led to increased self-esteem, community empowerment and enhanced community identity. Descriptions of individual museum projects discussed their positive impacts on health, educational achievements, unemployment and crime.

The GLLAM report advocated that museums maximise and sustain these efforts towards social inclusion. They encouraged museums to evaluate and document their work, in order to provide an evidence base that can be used to justify and inspire further projects. GLLAM also hoped to see a change in museum culture that would look upon museums as both a resource for social inclusion and as a facilitator that can enhance opportunities.[63] The perceived potential of museums to contribute to community development in general, and issues relating to exclusion in particular, is emphasised throughout the report. The GLLAM social inclusion report put this succinctly:

> The research shows that museums can not only tackle the four widely recognised key indicators linked to exclusion (health, crime, unemployment and education) but can also play a wider, and even, unique role in tackling disadvantage, inequality and discrimination.[64]

In this statement museums are established as places that can contribute to tackling some of the key causes of exclusion. The report is one example of numerous policy statements that emerged from the UK museum sector at this time, repeatedly endorsing the view that museums can contribute to such community problems.

Different ideas of social inclusion in other UK museum sectors

Although the term is well established, review of how inclusion was adopted by the museum sector shows that the notion, now widely accepted as a 'fuzzy concept',[65] is interpreted to reflect the needs of the contemporary context. Across the UK, inclusion work in museums is presented and used differently. This can be demonstrated by comparison of how social inclusion was interpreted in Scotland and Northern Ireland.

In Scotland the social inclusion strategy was embedded in an approach to tackle social justice. This is illustrated by the document *Museums and Social Justice: How Museums and Galleries Can Work for Their Whole Communities*, published in 2000 by the Scottish Museums Council (SMC). The SMC has adopted the term 'social justice' because, in its opinion, 'an individual's ability to participate fully in and have access to his or her cultural heritage is a matter of basic human right, not welfare'.[66] Reviewing the literature from the Scottish museums sector a number of conclusions can be drawn. Again, those in an advisory role within the museum sector have embedded themselves in Government policy. However, in practice, outcomes of the initiative show that the idea of justice in relation to museums may not have been taken up as fully as some of the documentation suggests. Finally, the term justice is understood differently across the Scottish Executive and the cultural sector.

In relation to the first point, use of the term justice by the SMC is a reflection of the context within which it is working. With the foundation of the Scottish Executive in 1999 a Minister for Social Justice was put in place with the remit to tackle injustice and poverty. This ministerial title suggests a more trenchant approach to social problems and possibly the more radical communitarian politics of Scotland compared to the rest of the UK. Within this context the idea was taken up by SMC with the production of a social justice strategy for the museum sector, which took the issues of inclusion and exclusion as its main themes. The strategy recommended steps towards a greater awareness of the local community and the profile of museum visitors, such as by undertaking an access audit and raising the awareness of social inclusion issues amongst staff. It also suggested museums should review displays, learning programmes and events in relation to inclusion. More recently, the SMC has continued this association with social justice by placing learning, within its learning and access strategy, in the context of social justice as a key Scottish Executive policy.[67] Within the Scottish context it has been suggested that this emphasis on social justice implies that issues such as access within museums should be promoted as an act of fairness or equality, rather than as part of a cultural welfare programme.[68]

Despite these examples, it is hard to tell if the notions of justice or inclusion have influenced practice in museums. Although *Museums and Social Justice* cites a number of examples of museums that have discussed their work in relation to the idea of justice, no reference to activity related to social justice or inclusion appears, for instance, in Annual Reviews of the National Museum of Scotland for 2002–3 and 2003–4. Furthermore, the term 'justice' makes no appearance in the *National Museum of Scotland Corporate Plan* for 2005–9 and inclusion only gets a brief mention.[69] In relation to how the term 'justice' is understood, for the SMC it is about rights of access. Scotland's *National Cultural Strategy* refers to justice as concerned with extending participation in disadvantaged areas.[70] In a review of the social and economic impacts of the arts and culture, published by the Education Department Research Programme of the Scottish Executive, social justice is discussed in relation to the reduction of offending behaviour and culture as a diversion from criminal behaviour.[71] In these three sources, three very different ideas of what justice is have been put forward; it is apparent that the idea of social justice is just as 'fuzzy' as social inclusion.

In Northern Ireland, policy development in relation to social inclusion in the museums sector is led by the Department of Culture, Arts and Leisure (DCAL), which is responsible for policy and administration of the museum, arts and cultural sector in Northern Ireland.[72] Here inclusion is forwarded in the context of what has been termed Targeting Social Need (TSN). This policy agenda was first launched in 1991 and has more recently been developed by the Office of the First Minister and Deputy First Minister (OFMDFM).[73] In the cultural context DCAL has produced its own *Targeting Social Need Action Plans*,[74] which reflect the priorities developed by the original TSN agenda and, since 1998, New TSN. The purpose of New TSN is to focus on unemployment and employability, and inequality in other policy areas, such as housing and education, and social inclusion. In relation to museums, the DCAL Action Plans for 2004–5 and 2005–6 have made the increase in participation by 'disadvantaged people' and increased awareness within the sector of minority ethnic groups the main objectives. Most recently OFMDFM have produced further strategies, such as an anti-poverty strategy, to which the cultural sector must respond. In Northern Ireland the museum sector has reacted to these policy areas by promoting awareness of work already underway in these areas and by developing new initiatives that relate to the field.[75] For many years local authority museums have worked closely with other council colleagues on social and community issues. For many, however, policy shifts and the introduction of new strategies, to which museums link out of both necessity and desire, are a constant challenge.

Critiques of community development approaches

In every case, approaches taken and responses to social policy relating to community development are determined by interpretations of the nature, causes and solutions of need. These interpretations will vary according to individual and party political positions on the matters. Therefore, we can never assume that the presentation of social policy is value free – social and political attitudes are inevitability embedded in the policy. There is the need, therefore, for those in the cultural sectors to be acutely aware of these influences and how the museum has been drawn into these new agendas. The social policy developments described in this chapter have been shaped by the New Labour agenda focus on communitarian ideals, which advocate higher levels of community participation and greater interest in community cohesion and regeneration. For many these ideals are welcome and they would say that such principles should pervade all areas of life and society. New Labour has, however, its share of critics. Those on the right argue that the goal may be appropriate but the understanding of why those difficulties arose, and how they should be resolved, is misunderstood. Critics on the left have welcomed communitarianism, but have criticised it for being ill conceived, authoritarian and, in the most part, focusing on maintaining a political position.

Adam Dinham describes the political approach to participation of the Labour Government as deriving from the principle of social capital and belief in the advantages of participation. He sees Labour approaches to participation as having three chief aims. The first he describes as the transformation of local people from passivity to responsibility. The second is the regeneration of disadvantaged areas by harnessing this new sense of responsibility in the service of targets for change. Thirdly, Dinham describes Labour as keen to engender a new relationship between the individual and the state that makes individuals 'stakeholders'. Dinham is critical of how this has been practised by Labour. He argues that their approach presumes that people are inactive, which contradicts the evidence for high levels of community activity in disadvantaged areas. He also believes that the purpose of Government initiatives is to stimulate community activity in the service of political aims, rather than empowering people according to their own terms. Finally, the Labour approach to participation is criticised as being led by the question of the relationship between state and society, rather than by people in their communities (which is the foundation of community development).[76]

Martin Hoban and Peter Beresford, for instance, have described how they looked forward to the introduction of the new policies for regeneration under the leadership of Prime Minister Tony Blair.[77] They welcomed the statements made on how new policies would lead to increased levels of community empowerment and participation in the regeneration process. The new policies focused largely on the introduction of local initiatives that would reverse economic decline that had led to increased poverty and unemployment. At the core of this approach was the introduction of greater levels of 'community self-help'[78] and the establishment of neighbourhood managers 'who would ensure neighbourhood renewal happens'.[79] Hoban and Beresford have found error with this method and suggest that the ideas at the core of these approaches need further thought. They argue that community development based on leadership could be a barrier to empowerment and participation, since to lead suggests that others will merely follow. They also state that self-help alone is not enough – its success depends on the opportunities provided. And, finally, the emphasis on neighbourhood development ignores the fact that economic decline may not be based on geographical area.

The adoption of the very idea of community has also been subject to question, never mind how it has been used to develop new policy practice. Martin Mowbray, for instance, discusses this in the terms of a 'return to vogue' of community in social policy. The new range of 'programmatic labels', such as community capacity building, government–community partnerships, community and neighbourhood renewal, now 'flourish in social policy discourse and government papers and speeches'.[80] He cites Gary Craig, who believes we should ask 'why governments have such enthusiasm for community development in the first place'.[81] Mowbray discusses examples of community building projects in Victoria, Australia, which have the unified feature of 'extravagant statements about aims and accomplishments'.[82] Mowbray refers to the 'loose and cynical use of community in social policy' and believes the term community is often used because of its 'aptitude for creating a positive regard for the organizations, policies or programmes to which it is applied'.[83] Programmes that are presented as bottom-up and directed at community self-determination are, he argues, instead 'funded and managed within centrally determined regulations'.[84]

Others have focused on the issue of maintenance of authority. Michael Marinetto argues that although communitarianism has led to greater public involvement in policy making, such as more public consultation, he believes this is presented within a very 'bounded structure' that maintains strong central control.[85] Isabelle Fremeaux, in her critique of the New Labour approach to community, questions how community is conceptualised. She notes that the idea of encouraging community development policy because of a belief in community 'characterized by harmony, affection, consensus and stability' overlooks the reality of 'coercion and power relations'.[86] She fears that 'the concept of community as promoted by New Labour is to be understood in moral terms, rooted in a discourse that easily slides into an authoritarian one'.[87] Brian Schofield believes we should move away from the idea of community as a descriptive concept and instead see it as part of a managerial process.[88] New Labour, he argues, has actively constructed and mobilised the discourse of community for the political aims of government. Using the concept of governmentality, as developed by Foucault, Schofield believes community is now a tool that enables governance and will naturalise and transfer political priorities.

Critique in the cultural sector

The debate regarding New Labour communitarianism is about issues of purpose and priorities – and these two concerns should also be used when considering the contribution of the cultural sector to social policy. We must ask on whose terms museum community involvement is being promoted – whether participation is being promoted to forward a Government agenda or whether it is being developed for the needs of the people. Within the museum sector we can ask whether are we adopting greater community awareness because our concern lies principally with the needs of community, or whether our interest begins with the museum and its development. In response, one would expect that those who have been trained in the area and have made a commitment to the museum sector would put the museum first. In that case, if community-related museum policy does not have the community at its origin, is it flawed?

61

We can consider such points when we review museum engagement with community development issues. For me these issues came to mind when reading some of the case studies described in *Museums and Galleries: Creative Engagement*, which was referred to at the beginning of this chapter. The example of workshops with youths in the National Museum of Photography, Film and Television was, for instance, justified because the young people might have been a threat to the collections and was regarded as a success because vandalism in the museum was reduced by 70 per cent and now the 'troublemakers' work in the museum. One can easily read this as an example of a social inclusion project being promoted for the need of the museum, rather than for the needs of the young people. The project was a success because the youths conformed to museum practice and the expectations museum staff have of their visitors. Of course, a reduction in vandalism is something we all espouse, but this seems to suggest that the priorities lay with the museum rather than with the communities the project targeted.

It is, however, the idea of linking social inclusion with museums that has raised most debate, and in this case we can focus our assessment on the idea of purpose. The loudest criticism of bringing the concerns of social inclusion into the cultural sector has come from the Institute of Ideas, a UK forum for debate that grew out of the *Living Marxism Magazine*.[89] Josie Appleton, writing in 2001 shortly after the publication of the GLLAM Report *Museums and Social Inclusion*, referred to the association as the 'politicisation of museums' and a 'disaster'. Criticism has also come from within the museum sector. Andrew Brighton, writing as senior curator of public programmes at Tate Modern in London, is also highly critical of the DCMS mandate to have museums concentrate efforts on social inclusion. Brighton suggests that it did not consider that the core activities of museums 'might be irreconcilable with the inclusion agenda'.[90] He accuses the DCMS of working to a purely political agenda with no care for the harm this might be causing museums. Questioning the aims of the DCMS research forum, he asks:

> Will the DCMS's research forum examine the harm done to cultural institutions by the social inclusion agenda? I think not. Has the DCMS and the government considered the ill-effects of enmeshing cultural institutions in their 'wider social and economic objectives'? Is it aware of the damage done to local authority museums and galleries by their absorption into the mainstream of leisure and amenity management?[91]

The numerous reports cited above provide an impression that culture is one of the key tools for community development in the UK, and indeed reports can be cited and examples of related projects can be presented that provide evidence of general acceptance of this point. A study undertaken by Andrew Newman and Fiona McLean, based on interviews with policy makers and practitioners, showed that despite a number of policy documents that have linked museums with the issue of social inclusion, in practice the connections are not so well made.[92] They identified a lack of policy coherence, adding that some were 'unquestioning in their belief that museums and galleries were powerful agents of social inclusion and social change, but were unable to identify how the process worked'.[93] Newman and McLean also found uncertainty within the museum sector of how to make the connection between their work and social inclusion objectives, as well as a lack of understanding of what is meant by social inclusion.

When evaluating the association between community and cultural policy it must be approached in two ways. In the first place it is necessary to have an understanding of how Government advocates the links between their policy priorities and culture. Secondly we must consider how those in the cultural sector respond to the challenge. It is useful to consider whether the link between culture and community policies has been initiated by Government, or if it is the cultural sector that has picked up on the new policies, and is promoting the link. In addition, the reaction from the cultural sector must also be broken down. The response of a Government-sponsored Department, such as the Department of Culture, Media and Sport, must be considered as significantly different from that of an independent museum body, such as the National Museum Directors' Conference or Centre Learning in Museums and Galleries. One would expect DCMS policy to be close to what the Government advocates, but one would hope that the latter would be more independent.

4

Social capital and the cultural sector

The discussion so far has shown that as approaches to community, and the practice of community development, shift so too will the nature of the involvement of museums. Museums, it is apparent, cannot be separated from the needs and concerns of other sectors. When national or local government sets its agenda, its priorities will shape museum policy and practice. When 'think tanks' produce reflection on key aspects of societal reform, whether in relation to education or social policy, they too will shift thinking about museums. An idea that is current amongst such national governments and think tanks is the notion of social capital, which has also found relevance for those exploring and developing the purpose of museums. In the US, for instance, social capital has been established as an important concept explored by the Saguaro Seminar, an initiative developed by Robert Putnam to reflect on trust and community engagement.[1] The concern of a meeting of the Seminar in 1999 was the role of the arts in civic engagement, which led to a set of recommendations on how the arts can be a means to develop social capital. In March 2006 the Institute for Public Policy Research (IPPR), 'the UK's leading progressive think tank', published a comment on cultural policy and civic renewal that took social capital as its key tool to explore the relationship between the two areas. Both of these initiatives, one American the other British, are a demonstration of a rising interest in the idea of social capital as relevant to how we plan for and think about culture, museums and heritage.

The reason why the notion of social capital, and how it has been related to the museum sector, is so interesting is because it has at its core a very particular idea of community and has developed its own approach to community development based on its notion of what is needed to establish a successful community. Many of the community development practices discussed in previous chapters do not carry an ideal notion of 'community', and how community should be fostered, quite so explicitly as found within the idea of social capital. The ideas of social cohesion, inclusion and participation, discussed in Chapter 3 for instance, are concerned with the improvement of the experience, conditions and change. Social capital, although also wishing to bring about change, brings with it an ideal of community, based on trust and reciprocity, which needs to be nurtured for the wellbeing of society. Within this context, museums, the arts and culture have become one of the means to create the bonds at the heart of a community rich in social capital.

The idea of social capital

Discussion of the concept of social capital has been common amongst economic, political and social science circles since the mid-twentieth century.[2] Our recent understanding, however, is derived from the work of contributors such as Pierre Bourdieu, James Coleman and Robert Putnam,[3] and has informed various public policy initiatives related to community capacity building, cohesion and partnerships.[4] The idea of social capital relates to theoretical discussions in the fields of sociology, education and economics, which have debated social action, as well as its impacts and potentials, in relation to the notion of 'capital'. In these contexts education or social action is discussed as a means to build social capital, and by doing so bring benefits to individuals within their communities. The idea of 'capital', which has its origins in economic theory, has itself been discussed in various ways. Pierre Bourdieu, for instance, presents the ideas of 'economic capital', 'cultural capital' and 'social capital'.[5] James Coleman, in addition to the idea of social capital, also discusses the formation of 'human capital'.[6] When the ideas of capital have been applied in the arts, museological and heritage fields they are either welcomed as a means to explore the potential impact of the culture or, sometimes, criticised as a concept formed on economic and capitalist principles that has no application in the cultural context. These differing responses also reflect the many tensions common in the cultural sector that arise from differing opinions regarding the purposes of heritage, arts and museums and so provide further stimulus for us to investigate the meaning of museums.

Bourdieu and capital

The writings of Pierre Bourdieu are often turned to as a means to explore how culture functions and the way different people respond to its presence. Again, his work is a means to explore the origins of the notion of capital and its eventual popularisation with the idea of social capital. For Bourdieu, cultural capital takes three forms. It is embodied through knowledge, objectified by the representation of cultural goods (such as pictures and books), and institutionalised, perhaps by educational achievements. Leading from this, social capital is defined by Bourdieu as 'membership of a group – which provides each of its members with the backing of the collectively owned capital'.[7] In other words, the benefits of cultural capital are passed on through the existence of social capital. Associations and connections within the network, and the material and symbolic exchanges that take place, benefit the members. For instance, connections between people can cause capital to be transferred from one person to another, such as the sharing of information through the casual exchange of knowledge. Positive benefits can also accrue from the act of social integration, which for some can be empowering. Furthermore, as argued by Bourdieu, cultural and social capital can later be converted to economic capital. The advantage of high levels of cultural and social capital can lead to further opportunities, and the confidence to take those up, which has economic benefits. It is also likely that cultural preferences and taste, as a form cultural capital, will shape economic and social opportunities as well as inequalities.[8]

The attraction and potential of heritage, culture and museums can be understood in relation to Bourdieu's theories of capital. The value of cultural capital is represented by the symbolic nature of objects and collections, whether these are in individual, community or national ownership. The possession of cultural capital can convey messages with regard to position and intellectual ability, as well as social and political viewpoints. Through objects a national museum can define its relationship with other nations; private collections can convey the wealth of the owner; and objects in personal ownership can represent the achievements, tastes and judgements of the holder. The possession of cultural capital is represented and constructed through the existence of such property – public display provides the opportunity to reinforce the message. The objects within collections forge a communal knowledge and create shared experiences. The national community, which constructs its identity with the aid of artefacts held in museums, uses this cultural capital to build connections between members, which in turn will foster social capital. Without even knowing the other members, a belief in their existence and the strength of their characteristics empowers the national community. Collections become the material evidence of other members of a community, past or present. The networks at the heart of the imagined community are united by common symbols and an agreed history that will, when embraced, produce the benefits associated with high levels of social capital. This highlights how cultural capital can operate at a national level by drawing on the resources of national museums and collections. Similar power structures can arise at the local level through community museums and their collections. As will be apparent through discussions in Chapter 7, which considers community museums in relation to social movements, the collections are used to convey messages about a particular community, reinforce beliefs and form connections. This is only done because the museum is a medium through which this can be achieved. The connections can be interpreted as forms of capital that convey messages about the bearer and will have further consequences. It is these outcomes, associated with the cultural capital of museums, which we need to be continually aware and critical of.

Putnam and contemporary ideas of social capital

Robert Putnam has investigated the idea of social capital and what he considers to be its decline in his book *Bowling Alone: The Collapse and Revival of American Community*.[9] Putnam used the bowling alley as an analogy for the loss of community in America – rather than bowling being a shared community activity it was becoming something people did by themselves. This change was interpreted as emblematic of how individuals are becoming isolated in society and the decline of group activity. Putnam traced a positive correlation between high levels of social capital and higher economic prosperity, better health, greater happiness, and superior educational outcomes. As a result, he advocates the development of social capital as a means to improve quality of life. The measure Putnam used in this investigation was based on a number of factors, including levels of community organisational life, individual engagement in public affairs and the existence of community voluntarism. He also considered informal sociability and levels of social trust. He argued that the existence of each of these factors, at high levels, created an integrated and networked community, with benefits passing from person to person through community contact. Putnam's approach has been summarised as:

> The social or community cohesion resulting from the existence of local horizontal community networks in the voluntary, state and personal spheres, and the density of networking between these spheres; high levels of civic engagement/participation in these local networks; a positive local identity and a sense of solidarity and equality with other community members; and norms of trust and reciprocal help, support and co-operation.[10]

The deliberate forging of the links, referred to by Putnam, has been coined in the term 'capacity building', which is understood as building capital where it is considered absent.[11] Community capacity is forged through various means: by creating partnerships between people and agencies; by enhancing perceptions of community cohesion; and by improving levels of participation in local management. It is considered that by greater links between levels in society, such as people of a particular area with their local government representatives, the ability for a community to achieve positive outcomes should be enhanced. The belief in increased participation of local groups, in how amenities should be managed or in the provision of facilities should lead to more appropriate use of resources and understanding between the various agencies.

Fostering social capital has become a frequent and popular policy issue – it is seen as a means to increase civic engagement and civic responsibility. By increasing community participation and enhancing community engagement, in various stages of local government, health promotion or education management, it is thought that more relevant and acceptable policy will be developed. In schools, for instance, using horizontal support networks (such as the buddy system) has been shown to decrease levels of bullying and truancy. Vertical networks, such as involving parents and community leaders in the establishment of a school culture/ethos, have also been considered a success.[12] In a study of how enhancement of social capital has been related to economic regeneration, researchers measured the level of social capital before and after community participation projects involving the redevelopment of derelict and under-used land on deprived estates in urban and rural Britain.[13] In this example social capital was measured on the basis of perceived levels of trust, participation in the form of voluntary activity, the use of community centres, and the general belief in the existence of community spirit. The study found that the regeneration scheme led to increased levels of social capital indicated by people having greater pride in their area, an enhanced community spirit, and a marked decrease in local crime.

The findings were used to argue that this form of community participation in local development is multi-beneficial. Social capital is here presented as something that has a range of benefits across a number of fields. In this example, the improvement of derelict land is not the key benefit; rather, the positive impact of personal and social change is considered to be the greater outcome.

Social capital and the cultural sector

It has already been well established that culture and the arts, especially in the UK, have been extensively investigated as a means to foster 'community economic development',[14] trigger social and economic regeneration,[15] and enhance levels of community participation.[16] Because of its global appeal, and how it unites many of these core ideas, the idea of social capital stands out from these earlier concerns. With examples emerging from the US, Australia and the UK, museum and heritage projects are being presented as an accessible means to develop the vertical and horizontal links associated with high levels of social capital. In an almost genial fashion, culture, the arts and heritage are being presented as a way of involving people in a non-threatening pursuit that can build the forms of capital necessary to forge community.

The examples of the Saguaro Seminar in 1999, and the recent IPPR report on social capital and cultural policy, provide some important indications of how it is thought the idea of social capital should be applied to the cultural sector. The *Better Together* report, published by the Saguaro Seminar in 2000, is the product of a belief that America is in 'civic crisis'[17] and only by building social capital will this be reversed. The section of the report that looks specifically at the role of the arts in building social capital cites numerous examples of arts projects and museum initiatives that have contributed to this end. The authors argue that the arts can nurture social capital by strengthening friendships, helping communities to understand and celebrate their heritage, and providing safe ways to discuss and solve difficult social problems. Examples of heritage and museum projects are given to illustrate their potential for providing a safe means of 'bridging differences', 'resolving community conflict' and nurturing 'community healing'.[18] For fear that participation in the arts is waning, and because of the potential of arts for rebuilding community, the *Better Together* report recommended three principles that ought to guide the arts: encourage initiatives that form bridges across race, income, gender, religion and generation; return to the arts as the basis of community organisations, such as a music hall; and include arts and culture in planning for the community. It states that these principles should be supported by increased funding for the sector; greater collaboration between sectors; increased civic dialogue; including the arts in 'social problem solving'; and using the arts as a community service.[19] The sentiment at the heart of this report is much like what was emerging from the UK at a similar time. Like the social inclusion agenda in the UK, the concern is with building bridges, the arts are regarded as a community service, and the idea of collaboration is forwarded. However, these ideas are extended to become a means to build, or sometimes rebuild, a community ideal.

Social capital has been taken up by the museum profession as a means to demonstrate the value of museums. This is well illustrated in an example of a community learning project at the Parramatta Heritage and Visitor Information Centre in New South Wales, Australia.[20] In this example Genelle Sharrock, the Education and Public Programs Officer, advances museums as a means to nurture and grow social capital. By putting people first at the Heritage Centre, and developing preschool learning activities and craft workshops for adults, she believes they have generated 'observable and tangible social capital outcomes'. Both the preschool activities and the craft workshops allowed people who were usually non-museum goers to make use of the Centre. Development of the programmes resulted from staff directly asking the groups what they wanted from the Centre. Sharrock describes opportunities for people to make new social connections as a result of attending the new activities. She saw evidence of greater reciprocity and trust when established participants introduced and welcomed newcomers, and as a result of higher levels of familiarity between tutors and Centre staff. The Heritage Centre also became a place for those for whom English was a second language to improve their language skills and build confidence. Sharrock presents the learning programmes as a means to build social capital and she interrogates their value according to the features of social capital. By doing so Sharrock demonstrates how this relatively new approach to understanding the impact of cultural programmes is being used to understand the meaning and potential of the museum visit. For Sharrock, the value of the social capital approach is that it emphasises the subtle benefits, central to the idea of capital, which may otherwise be overlooked by assessors of the impact of the museum visit. Through such analysis the range of consequences or opportunities arising from acquiring cultural assets through engagement with arts, museums or heritage is acknowledged. For the advocates of social capital in the cultural sector, it provides a better awareness of the value of cultural activity for improving self-confidence, enhancing wellbeing and developing positive relationships. Without that awareness, many would argue, we are likely not to appreciate the full effect of the museum visit.

In the UK, interest in the idea of social capital, and its application in the cultural sector, has not yet reached the same level of debate or acceptance as the notion of social cohesion or cultural diversity. Recently social capital has only been mentioned now and then, whereas the others have become commonplace. However, a number of reports of the past few years indicate that the idea has gone from the occasional mention to a greater level of establishment. As this has happened it is evident the saliency of the term is also on the increase. In 2001 the series of briefing papers *Recognising Culture*, published in partnership by Comedia, the Department of Canadian Heritage and UNESCO, included an essay on the subject of culture and social capital.[21] In 2002 *Creative Engagement* made brief mention of the idea of social capital in its comment on the value of museums, arguing that museums and galleries are a means to 'create social capital, educating and empowering individuals and groups alike, creating networks and stimulating dialogue'.[22] This report, however, did not go into any depth about the meanings of the term. In 2004 the Department of Culture,

Media and Sport funded a literature review to consider the role of social capital in the cultural sector.[23] Most recently, in May 2006, the Institute for Public Policy Research, a UK think tank, issued a report dedicated to the associations between cultural policy, social capital and civic renewal. However, despite this greater use of the term in cultural literature, none has fully embraced the associations, contradictions and potential difficulties with the idea.

Each of these studies demonstrates that the cultural sector is being considered according to a new variable. In the working paper published through Comedia, social capital is presented in positive language as concerned with 'a community's human wealth' whose assets are the skills and capacities of each community, which can be enhanced through engagement in cultural activity.[24] The DCMS literature review explored the relevance of the cultural sector for building social capital and, drawing on past research, demonstrated a positive relationship. The IPPR report also found that cultural activity can be used to build social capital and foster civic renewal, and recommended policy goals to nurture this potential. Here, culture is described as a means for communities to develop skills and rebuild community, a stepping-stone to becoming an engaged citizen, and a means to create trust. Approaches are recommended that will place thinking about social capital and civic renewal at the core of cultural policy develop-ment, which will be put into practice by encouraging greater participation.[25] Finally, the idea of social capital is also being used as a means to reflect upon the museum visit. Andrew Newman and Fiona McLean, for instance, described museum-based community initiatives that have enhanced civic involvement and successfully built social capital in a place that had formerly 'lost its community spirit'.[26] They present social capital as 'a pragmatic way to understand the impact of the museum experience upon visitors ... and museum-based community development projects'.[27]

It seems that social capital could be emerging as another policy area that cultural activity could be associated with and evaluated according to. For many there is an easy association between the factors that build social capital and the potential impacts of cultural participation. For those in the cultural sector who are keen on the idea, the notion appeals because it takes account of a whole range of long-term benefits of cultural participation, which might otherwise have gone unaccounted. In the first instance, a visit to a museum or participation in a workshop will bring the immediate benefit of enjoyment and learning, but now cultural managers can also refer to the unseen benefits gained from the creation of networks, trust and confidence. It seems that social capital could be the idea that, when applied to the cultural sector, really opens up how we think about the benefits of cultural participation. At last, there might be greater appreciation of the breadth of consequences of cultural activity, which may mean that culture and the arts are more fully embraced and nurtured. This is a goal that advocates of the arts, culture and museums aspire to; however, is social capital the vehicle by which we should bring this about? Despite so many positive claims for the idea, research that has gone further, to look in greater depth at the idea of social capital, provides a more thorough awareness of potential problems with the idea, which gives us a far greater understanding of the nature of the concept. So, in relation to our interest in museums, there are two concerns we should have: is the idea of social capital helpful and can culture be applied to the concept to foster positive outcomes?

The critique of social capital and its application to culture

Its advocates may plausibly present the concept of social capital, but there is a fierce body of literature that is prepared to question the fundamentals of the idea. Indeed, the writing that describes how the possession of social capital can lead to greater empowerment, raise skill levels and improve opportunities is attractive; however, one cannot ignore the literature that asks us to look more critically at the concept.[28] Michael Foley and Bob Edwards, who are amongst the most fervent critics of the Putnam idea of social capital, state that all too often 'the renewal of civil society and the generation of social capital within it are accepted uncritically as offering a panacea to contemporary social ills'.[29]

Awareness of the potential problems with social capital ranges from those who still believe it is useful, but recommend an understanding of the dangers that may be associated with it, to those who passionately argue against current inter-pretations of the notion. Alan Kay, for instance, presents social capital as a means for enhanced community development strategies through a better under-standing of how communities operate. He also presents the limitations of the idea: 'binding the community into a cohesive unit can make a community more isolated and less tolerant'; networks can have an adverse effect on equal opportunities; and he argues it can be used to further personal ends.[30] Elsewhere, studies have argued that the goal of a so-called cohesive civic community, with high levels of social capital and characterised by generalised levels of trust and identity (i.e. trust people you haven't met), has been criticised as 'romanticised and inaccurate'.[31] And the very idea that people should strive for membership of community-based organisations has been criticised as unrealistic to modern life-styles. The bridging function of social capital, as presented by Putnam, has been challenged on the basis of the potentially harmful effect of community bonding. The creation of such bonds could be used to reinforce homogeneity amongst the community, defining the outsiders and leading to exclusion. Catherine Camp-bell, for instance, warns that 'cohesive communities might be characterised by distrust, fear, racism, exclusion of outsiders, and as such may not be healthy for those who are not part of them or for insiders who disagree with the majority'.[32] The most fervent critics of social capital argue that Putnam has ignored the power relations at the core of social capital, its dependence on the success of capitalism, and the political value of its promotion. Rather than being the basis of altruism, social capital is interpreted as a concept based on competitiveness, the possession of power, and retaining the position of power.

Those whose concern is with the power relations at the core of social capital argue that the idea is based on a capitalist agenda. Vicente Navarro writes that for social capital the purpose of social action 'is reduced to accumulating more capital so that the individual can compete better' and presents the contradiction that the observed lack of togetherness 'may be rooted precisely in the existence of capitalism and competitiveness'.[33] For instance, lack of unionisation in the United States, Navarro believes, is more an indication of class and political power than a lack of voluntarism or community. He also believes that community-based initiatives can lead to unjust systems.[34] Navarro goes on to argue that the idea of social capital popularised by Putnam is embedded with values that run contrary to the goal of solidarity, principally because of the political purpose underpinning the desire to grow social capital. James DeFilippis provides very clear arguments about why we cannot easily assume that social capital (as promoted by Putnam) is at the core of the promotion of civil engagement, economic growth and democratic government.[35] Emphasising the value of Bourdieu, DeFilippis sees capital as concerned with the possession of power. Criticising Putnam, DeFilippis rejects the idea that communities can possess social capital and instead sees communities as the outcome or product of sets of power-laden relationships (based on social issues, politics, culture and economics). For DeFilippis, improvement of conditions for the poor is more likely to occur if power relations are changed, rather than connections increased (arguing that even by making connections people can still be 'kept in their place'). Greater awareness of power relations leads to better understanding of the impact of group and volunteer activity – all is not necessarily equal. DeFilippis gives the example of participation in a Chamber of Commerce as having a different impact in comparison with involvement in a local union. Considering the issue of networks in relation to economic development, DeFilippis states simply 'if everyone is connected, then everyone by definition would lose the benefits of those connections because they would no longer gain capital from them'; furthermore, 'if the social capital in question is a network that helps people find employment, it would clearly be in the interest of those realizing and appropriating the social capital to keep the network as closed as possible'.[36] If the idea of social capital is to be of value, DeFilippis advocates social networks that allow people access to capital and the power to control that capital.

Foley and Edwards largely ask us to think again about the over-simplified idea of social capital provided in the work of Putnam, arguing that emphasis on the importance of trust, the establishment of norms and shared values, and the creation of a 'civic culture' is misguided.[37] They emphasise the point that the 'use value' of these factors is context dependent and means different things according to the person, place and time. Because of these variations they believe that levels of trust, for instance, cannot be measured, evaluated and usefully compared as an indicator of improved experiences or conditions. Furthermore, the existence of trust or networks will have varied outcomes – maybe in the short term a network can bring benefits but this may not be the case in the longer term. Foley and Edwards prefer an idea of social capital that acknowledges the importance of access and, crucially, the resources to make use of opportunities. They promote greater awareness of context, and stress the fact that not all resources are equally available and that not everyone makes full use of the social capital available to them (so social capital may exist but not be of benefit).

For these critics it is not an outright rejection of the idea of social capital; instead it is often a recommendation that we should be 'very careful about how we define and use the term'.[38] What can be gathered from the studies that have criticised simplistic and overly optimistic ideas of the notion is that we must be clear that it is not just about developing networks and trust; rather, the value lies in addressing power relationships and access to opportunity.

The application to culture

Some of the warnings of the potentially negative impacts of social capital are even evident in Sharrock's very positive account of how the Parramatta Heritage Centre contributed to the growth of social capital. Sharrock refers to the pre-school programmes as so successful that when one child graduates a younger sibling often immediately fills its place. This suggests a form of lineage is beginning to be associated with the programmes. In addition, she describes how the 'regulars' have developed a strong sense of ownership of the programme, so that when new people joined, and the group became too large, 'they felt the quality of "their" experience was threatened'.[39] Both of these points suggest that a group is forming such a tight bond around these museum programmes that the established participants could be beginning to exclude non-members. As the group bonds, it begins to protect its particular identity and relationships that have formed through established connections.

In the Parramatta example we are made aware of the power relations of groups and what purpose that might be put to. More fundamentally, when culture is engaged as a means to build social capital, we need to address not only the concept of social capital being used, but also the version of culture that is integrated with it. In each case, we need to ask questions about what form 'culture' has taken and what are its impacts. The glowing reports on the benefits of culture, common in government publications from the sector, often come across as simplistic and over-generalised. For example, the tendency for culture to be defined and presented in an elitist fashion, which can lead to further exclusion or inequality, is often overlooked. Some recognition of this is found but, in most cases, this is dismissed as avoidable if we remain 'geared towards positive outcomes'.[40]

Taking our cue from the issues raised about social capital, and how it has been adopted, we can also evaluate the idea of culture and its application. First, the presentation of culture is very much a product of power relations. These power relations can be oppressive, exclusionary and disempowering. Culture can be used to maintain difference, preserve class structures and legitimise the possession of power. The example of the Asian Civilisation Museum in Singapore is used by Helena Bezzina, of the National Museum of Australia, as a means to demonstrate the negative uses of cultural capital. The Museum tells the story of the Peranakan people in Singapore through the exhibition 'Peranakan Legacy' that opened in 2000. The exhibition, Bezzina argues, is used to endorse the Government's attempts at developing a particular national identity for Singapore and to forward the official 'apolitical' way of displaying Peranakan culture as bygone and exotic. She believes the museum is encouraged to use the cultural capital it possesses to conform to the state's 'authoritarian, non-discursive discourse on national identity and stability'.[41] Even the formation of networks between people and communities and the museum or cultural sector (e.g. through community consultation) may not lead to a reversal of such relationships. One could even argue that the fully connected museum, led and managed by the community, will not necessarily lead to greater opportunity. Navarro argued that in some cases federal projects were more just than community-based initiatives, and this could also be the case in the management and presentation of heritage. Foley and Edwards emphasise the importance of understanding differences in context when thinking about social capital. Again, one should not generalise about the impact of culture and think that we can move from one place to another and assess it according to set values.

What seems to be absent in the UK studies on the links between social capital and cultural policy is any exploration of the contested, divisive and conflict-ridden nature of culture, arts and heritage. Although the fact that culture is itself a contested notion does get recognition, the use of culture as a tool to divide and separate gets little or no acknowledgement. This is most obvious in Helen Gould's description of the value of culture to community. She comments on the value of a community coming together to 'share cultural life, through celebration, rites and intercultural dialogue', which she argues enhances 'its relationships, partnerships and networks – in other words, developing social capital'.[42] These positive interpretations are also to be found amongst those attempting to promote culture activity that others might find oppressive. In Northern Ireland such sentiment has been used as justification for the continuation of controversial marches by the Protestant Orange Order: the Order argues that this is a celebration of their culture, a valued right, and one that helps build community identity and networks.[43] The recent re-presentation of the marches as 'festivals' is presented as a means to invite wider acceptance. In this example the promotion of culture has negative connotations for some sections of the Northern Ireland population. To be fair, Gould does go on to mention briefly that culture is contested; however, the brevity of that reference is common amongst many of the studies. Furthermore, in such studies, the very idea of heritage is also under-conceptualised. What is not acknowledged is that heritage is always an invented notion, one that is constructed with some contemporary purpose in mind. As a result, we cannot generalise about its altruistic possibilities. Heritage will always be formed in a way that forwards the agendas of those involved in its construction.

Given the critique of the idea of social capital, the issue is not whether those engaged in museum projects based around the idea of enhancing social capital are maliciously involved in a capitalist campaign, or are keenly trying to maintain established power relations – I am sure the majority are not. Rather, my concern is whether engaging in the social capital objective is a worthwhile use of their talents and whether it is allowing us truly to value the purpose and potentials of museums.

Social capital and civic engagement in practice: the Museums and Community Initiative of the American Association of Museums

In 2002 the American Association of Museums (AAM) issued a challenge to the museum sector to 'master civic engagement'. This challenge was the result of the Museums and Community Initiative, which had been exploring the relationship between museums and community and the potential of museums to foster community. It is particularly useful to analyse this initiative in the light of thinking in relation to social capital. Civic engagement is at the core of social capital, and the concern with community, central to the Museums and Community Initiative pursued by the AAM, reflects the emphasis given to the notion of community as found within social capital. In contrast to the UK museum sector, direct recommendation for museum policy concerning what museums can do for cultural diversity, inclusion or cohesion is not found in the US case. Instead the AAM explores community by expanding the civic role of museums and enabling greater community–museum engagement. Discussions as part of this programme were concerned with how museums relate to their communities, how museums should respond to changes amongst communities, and the new opportunities that have arisen from this. The key recommendations of the initiative were centred on developing means for museums to become what the Association refers to as more civically engaged and community conscious.

The American Association of Museums

The AAM describes itself as the national service organisation that represents the American museum sector and addresses the needs of museums to enhance their ability to serve the public interest.[44] The challenge to master civic engagement was described by the Chair of the Board of Directors as a means to 'revisit the power of community', and to consider what assets the sector has to add to the shared enterprise of 'building and strengthening community bonds'.[45] This national commitment to the development of community originated from an 'experiment' launched in 1998 that involved museums and community groups in Philadelphia working together as a means for the museum sector to get a better awareness of its social and educational potential.[46] The findings of this process later formed the basis of the report *Museums in the Life of a City*, which traced the methods used and provided an evaluation of the scheme. The Philadelphia scheme was followed in 1998 with the 'Museums and Community Initiative', which was regarded as a means to strengthen the relationship between museums and their communities across the US. Leading on from the Museums and Community Initiative, the AAM published *Mastering Civic Engagement* (2002), which provided a number of recommendations based on the findings of the Museums and Community Initiative. Central to these recommendations was an assessment of the core principles museums should embrace in the future. These were named as greater civic engagement, democracy and community building. The call to 'master civic engagement' was part of the final dissemination stage that attempted to share best practice for creating and strengthening bonds between museums and others.

It is significant that at the end of the 1990s 'community' was placed at the core of the work of the AAM. The rationale for the programme was based on a particular interpretation of the conditions of contemporary society and how people should respond. Robert Archibald, Chair of the Museums and Community National Taskforce, portrays this in his outline of the rationale. He justifies the links between museums and community because of the need for increased democratisation, resulting from the negative impacts of globalisation, as well as the existence of a 'crisis in community'. He identifies 'disastrous results' deriving from the loss of 'location and neighbourhood', which he states has had 'wretched consequences'. He describes these as the reduction of distinctiveness of place and the loss of cultural identity. He believes these have been caused by the commodification led by the market, or by the fact that cultural identity has been 'crushed in the blender of mass culture'.[47] Christopher Gates, President of the National Civic League and Special Expert Advisor to the Initiative, opens his assessment of the role of museums and community with reference to the tragedy of September 11, 2001. Museums, he argues, must more than ever re-examine the role they play in strengthening democracy, encouraging civic engagement and forming better communities.[48] It is impossible to read such assessments, which in themselves would engender fear and foreboding, without thinking of the writings of Zygmunt Bauman. Bauman believes that increased interest in the idea of community has been generated by a rising sense of insecurity and threat. He argues that community has been claimed as a means to reverse uncertainty because it is thought to bring protection and wellbeing. It seems that here again, as in the examples discussed from the UK, community is the panacea that will retrieve an ideal and link us to a better society.

Description of the Museums and Community Initiative

Through the Museums and Community Initiative the US museum sector was asked to respond to the 'crisis in community' so as to ensure their 'continued productive existence' and to make a contribution to community and environmental sustainability. The vision was for the museum sector to contribute to the development of community in the twenty-first century, a community that would have 'an inclusive narrative that encompasses people and their place and defines common values and shared aspirations'.[49] The principles underpinning the Museums and Community Initiative provide us with an impression of how museums were being profiled during this period. The key idea underpinning the initiative was to encourage museums to become more embraced in 'community life'. Museums are described by AAM as 'cultural symbols', and by exploring the relationship between museums and community the Initiative aimed to demonstrate the means to greater community engagement.

The Initiative took the form of a number of recorded dialogues between community representatives and their museum colleagues across the US during 2000 and 2001, which were to inform museum policy and change. These were held in six cities across America and more than 700 people participated, 35 per cent representing museum leadership and 65 per cent coming from community organisations.[50] The community dialogues were held with people described as responsible for 'building community, serving communities and linking communities and museums' – the invited participants were an impressive array of directors and executive directors of various agencies. The goals for the dialogues were a reflection of the perceived needs of society and of museums within that. The first was identified as to 'explore an expanded civic role for museums in building social capital and contributing to community life'; the second, to 'discuss creative strategies for effective community–museum engagement'; and the third, to 'establish a framework for continuing conversations about community–museum relationships'.[51]

The resulting dialogues revealed the forces that are barriers both to the creation of community and to the development of museums as community spaces. In the dialogues museums were described as 'not community places', as 'not familiar' and as having 'physical and metaphorical barriers'. Participants observed a 'rift' between what museums represent and what communities expect museums to present.[52] Museums were accused of provoking 'feelings of incompetence' as well as being passive and lacking interaction.[53] Participants also observed a 'failure to listen' to the community amongst museums.[54] Repeated references were also made to a lack of trust amongst communities for museums. These assessments are unrecognisable in comparison to the more positive view of the community value of museums that came from those within the sector. The AAM Board of Directors, for instance, described museums as 'community cornerstones' that contribute to community enterprise, transform how people view the world, and foster life-long learning and the expression of different points of view.[55] The community dialogues certainly provided evidence to challenge that view and they reveal the danger associated with generalising on the experience of museums.

These community dialogues show a consensus amongst the participants about a loss of community, and an agreement that museums can make a positive contribution. Examples of encouraging experiences were used as justification that museums can be reinvented in an attempt to reverse long-established negative associations. In most cases the groups found that communities were divided because of experiences of geography, language, population change and perceptions of cultural difference. Communities also felt aliened from established systems, and feared crime and intolerance.[56] The groups recommended how museums might contribute to overcoming these experiences. They suggested museums should listen to constituencies and demystify the museum. Museums should include more stories, histories and cultures that are relevant, 'so people can find themselves there'.[57] The importance of building trust was emphasised, as well as of forming meaningful partnerships that would cause a re-evaluation of the museum idea.

According to many social commentators, from the politician to the academic campaigner (such as Putnam), these wants are what we are all seeking, or at least should be looking for. Repeatedly, policy documents and guidance notes are telling us that we need to know we are of relevance or valued, feel included, and experience high levels of trust and meaningful partnerships. The aspirations of the Museums and Community Initiative have become intertwined with the ambitions of popular political and social projects. The museum initiative was a reflection of its time and cut across the needs and experiences of people in a range of contexts to be voiced in connection with the museum. The project was so much of its time, of 1998–2002, that four years later there is no mention of it on the AAM website and links between current initiatives and this earlier programme are barely made.

Creating the community conscious museum

The core recommendation of the AAM Initiative is for the museum sector to become more community conscious – this is presented as valuable both for the community itself and for the museum sector. Robert Archibald, Chair of the National Task Force, sees museums as 'places of dialogue, advocates of inclusion, places of value and incubators of community'.[58] The feedback produced from the dialogues must have been useful for museum staff to understand how some people see museums, and to make them realise that museums may not be as community conscious as, or indeed the incubators, we might like to think they are. What the Initiative has demonstrated for those who are interested in understanding the place of museums, and how those who are influential in the sector approach them, is that they are given grand purpose – the essays emerging from the scheme are rarely modest or cautious about what they say about museums. Neither does this prudence extend to the ideal of community, which is continually championed.

In this Initiative museums and community are presented as having a natural association – because both are good for society. In this presentation both are elevated to a position where they should be revered. Neither is thoroughly challenged, at least from the perspective of our fundamental understanding of one or the other. The negative experience of museums, provided at some of the dialogues, is not the beginning it should be to really exposing the failures of museums and their potential inadequacies. Teamed with a concept that is as difficult and precarious as community, caution should reign. Instead, drawing on the idea of the value of a strong, united community, the museum is presented as a place that can foster well-being, bring people together and improve our health. The questions that the programme engaged with included whether museums can 'consciously build social capital' and 'create a strong, positive sense of place'. They also asked whether museums can 'unite disparate parts of the community in constructive ways and build trust' and 'engage in the issues that influence or shape the community's health or well-being'.[59] No concrete answer or means to achieving these outcomes is provided – maybe that would have been beyond the scheme. Rather, what we find is the forging of an attitude to museums amongst those within the sector.

Never mind the transformation of community, which is the goal of community development initiatives that the sector has twinned with: transformation of the museum is the key message of the Museums and Community Initiative. The dialogues raise the issue of whether the AAM museum and community initiative is most concerned with the revival of community or with the survival of the museum. The two agendas are subtly interwoven – with museums presented as a means to forge community and the involvement of community as an opportunity to improve the relevance and sustainability of museums. Ellen Hirzy is quite open in her belief that a museum's fiscal health relates to its community endorsement and that the museum must master civic engagement because the task is 'critical to their evolution, their relevance and their survival'.[60] The dual purpose of revival and survival should not be a surprise; and one could argue that it is unlikely to cause harm. However, it does suggest that when engaging with community the museum sector does not have an altruistic agenda. Just as people seek community when they are looking for security in an insecure world, museums also pursue community when they need to reassess their roles and their futures.

The purpose of the AAM Initiative was civic engagement – the idea of 'the civic' is at the core of social capital. This is how social capital is presented by Putnam, has been understood by the AAM, and has been adopted elsewhere. For Putnam, endorsing the civic will revive American community. For AAM, museums are a means for a community to become more civically engaged and the recent initiative an opportunity for museums to become more involved with their communities. In the UK, the Institute for Public Policy Research, in its discussion of cultural policy and social capital outlined at the beginning of this chapter, refers to civic renewal, civic participation and civic trust. In the discussion of social capital earlier in this chapter, the various commentators I have drawn from twin the idea of civic with concepts of engagement, renewal, participation, responsibility, involvement and the creation of a cohesive civic community. They refer to those who believe in 'civic crisis' and the formation of 'civic culture'. In relation to museums and culture, the sectors have been asked to embrace the civic role of museums and place civic renewal 'at the heart of its outlook'.[61]

In these interpretations community and the civic are brought together, civic participation is presented as a form of community engagement, and active citizens are advocated as people who create communal ties. However, it is essential to understand the difference between 'civic' and 'community' and what the terms imply. Contemporary ideas of our civic role, drawing from the communitarian ideal, are concerned with our contribution to civil society and link to the idea of citizenship. The civic structures are those of public life, such as state and government, and are an expression of our relationship with that. Community, as discussed in Chapter 2, can have a different emphasis and for some it will be formed on the basis of place, history and social ties. Community can exist outside state structures, and perhaps it is important that it should do so. Recently the idea of a 'civic community', which has been so popularised by political leaders, has combined the two ideas and is perhaps using the positive connotations often associated with the term community to give civic goals, as defined by Governments, a warmer glow. So when we think that museums and culture are being asked to engage with their communities, we need to think of the context and purpose that is underpinning this move. Is it the community of different interest groups who have come together for their own reasons; or is it the civically-engaged community who will become more involved in civic society and, as a result, become better citizens as defined by the structures of government?

5

Museums, cultural diversity and multiculturalism

The International Council of Museums (ICOM) policy statement on museums and cultural diversity presents, as one of its ten key issues, the statement that 'museums have increasingly become forums for the promotion of community relations and peace' and says:

> In addressing the problems of the world created due to inadequate cross cultural understanding, historical fears and ethnic tensions, museums are increasingly connecting with the important role that they can play in the promotion of cultural understanding through negotiated activities driven by community relations strategies.[1]

The ICOM call, made in 1997, for museums to become places to address cultural understanding, historical fears and ethnic tensions was very much a sign of the times. The twentieth century proved that historical reference can be used as a means to forge ethnic tensions and heighten fear. Perhaps we should now use our heritage infrastructure to address that. It is through adopting cultural diversity and multiculturalism policy, and linking it to the work of museums, that many think we can use museum collections to explore difference in a constructive manner. As a result, globally the ideas of cultural diversity, multiculturalism and the promotion of good relations are influencing how we develop museum policy and plan new initiatives. When reading the terms, and using them to shape how we think about museums, it is important to keep in mind that they have different origins and subtleties and should not (although it often happens) be used interchangeably. It is also important to be aware that people can use the same words with different intentions. In relation to multiculturalism, for instance, some will prefer the term used as the description of a situation, or lived experience, such as a multicultural society, but will not endorse it as a state ideology.[2]

Internationally, museums, heritage and culture have become intertwined with the community relations agenda broadly, and multiculturalism and cultural diversity in particular. This chapter explores some of the ways that museums have become forums for the promotion of good community relations, mainly through associating with cultural diversity thinking and policy. It falls into two parts: the first unpicks the ideas of cultural diversity and multiculturalism, and the second considers this in relation to museum practice. The discussion of multiculturalism looks to how the heritage and museum sectors have become a means to implement policy in this area and it also places this in the context of the continual debate on the value of that policy. Examples of museum initiatives are used, in the second part of the chapter, to illustrate the impact of this on museum policy.

In comparison with the concerns of community cohesion, social inclusion and social capital, which were discussed in previous chapters, the concern of multi-culturalism, and its application to improving understanding and relations between people, is a far more established practice. As a result there is a longer history of debate between the concepts, which have evolved since their profile was raised with some of the earliest policies of the 1970s. The literature is rich both in favour of the adoption of multiculturalism and against it. The resulting debate has been highly influential and, because of the overlap between various social policy areas, has consequences for approaches to related areas. For instance, opinion regarding multiculturalism, both as an idea and as a policy, will also impact on attitudes to cohesion or inclusion. Getting to grips with the debate in multiculturalism, and its impact on the museum sector, has a very important opinion-making role for other areas.

Understanding the ideas

Community relations cannot be understood in any one way. Largely used to refer to the relationships between different groups, and most often those seen to be of different ethnic or racial origins from the majority, it has been recently associ-ated with ideas of cultural diversity, multiculturalism and pluralism. This is the case if you look at the history of race relations in the United States, the rise of multiculturalism in Canada, and issues relating to identity, belonging and movement of people in Europe. In different instances diversity is often twinned with the word cultural and is sometimes used interchangeably with the idea of multiculturalism. Those who have distinguished between the terms refer to diversity as the expression of difference and multiculturalism as the ordering of this difference into recognised ways of living. Established as a term that refers to people of different ethnic or racial origin living amongst a majority, cultural diversity is increasingly being used to take account of sexuality, disability and the socially excluded.[3] As individuals we are all different; in a multicultural society that difference is considered as part of shared communities. The ideology of multiculturalism has been popularised as a means to foster public recognition and respect of difference, different values, beliefs and lifestyles. As a political tool it has become a policy approach used to manage cultural difference, and an attempt to reduce racial tension and increase understanding between communities.

The importance of the recognition and acceptance of diverse cultures for peace and prosperity underpins the UNESCO Universal Declaration on Cultural Diversity adopted in November 2001,[4] which was then furthered in the

Convention on the Protection and Promotion of the Diversity of Cultural Expressions agreed in October 2005. In both instances cultural diversity is described as 'the common heritage of humanity' and the 2005 Convention emphasises its desire for the promotion of democracy, tolerance, social justice and mutual respect.[5] This builds on a legacy of cultural and human rights policy put forward by UNESCO since its foundation. Appreciation and understanding of cultural diversity is given a purpose: the 2001 Declaration opens by presenting itself as a means for states to 'reaffirm their conviction that intercultural dialogue is the best guarantee of peace'; and the 2005 Convention affirms that this is 'indispensable for peace and security at the local, national and international levels'.[6]

A sense of what UNESCO is promoting is evident in some of the principles it has adopted (see Table 5.1).[7] The principles are expressed in the context of a belief that culture, in all forms, should be approached as the heritage of humanity – the expression, recognition and preservation of which is considered a human right. By doing so we are contributing to creativity, solidarity and sustainable human development. It is these ideas that have been integrated into museum policy internationally, shaping museum practice in relation to appointments, collecting and exhibitions as well as opinions regarding the role of museums in society. Although predating the above UNESCO policy, the general approach is also to be found in the ICOM *Museums and Cultural Diversity Policy Statement*, produced in 1997 by the Working Group on Cross Cultural Issues. This statement puts forward some of the key areas that link to how museums should be thinking about diversity. In its overview of findings, the ICOM statement calls for 'equity of access' and 'higher levels of excellence'. It makes the appeal that cultural diversity is the 'rich inheritance of humanity that will endure as the central pillar for peace, harmony and cultural sustainability'. This involves 'a fundamental need to acknowledge that all cultures and their manifestations are equally valid in a culturally democratic world'. The ICOM principles also advocate an 'inclusive museology' that would include increasing awareness of the cultural

Table 5.1 Principles selected from the UNESCO Universal Declaration on Cultural Diversity (2002)

Culture takes diverse forms across time and space. This diversity is embodied in the uniqueness and plurality of the identities of the groups and societies making up humankind . . . [Culture] is the common heritage of humanity and it should be recognised and affirmed.

In our increasingly diverse societies, it is essential to ensure harmonious interactions among people and groups with plural, varied and dynamic cultural identities as well as their willingness to live together. Policies for inclusion and participation of all citizens are guarantees of social cohesion, the vitality of civil society and peace.

The defence of cultural diversity is an ethical imperative, inseparable from respect for human dignity. It implies a commitment to human rights and fundamental freedoms.

Cultural rights are an integral part of human rights

needs of minorities and the adoption of museum management practices that better address cultural pluralism. Furthermore, museums should make themselves relevant to 'new generations' and the 'concerns of government'.

It will be useful now to consider the above sentiment in context of the debate regarding cultural diversity and multiculturalism. Fuelling that debate, Brian Barry, author of *Culture and Equality*, argues that multiculturalism 'poses as many problems as it solves'.[8] He suggests that such policies make the goal of egalitarianism more difficult because they weaken minority groups, cause tension between groups, and lessen liberal protection for individuals. On the subject of culture, Barry's critique of multiculturalism also calls into question the justification of cultural practices, as a valued part of a heritage, which may have negative connotations for others. He refers to this as an example of the 'abuse of culture'. For Barry, using the claim of 'culture' as a defence for certain activities is not acceptable, as is the belief that preservation of a group's culture is essential to its wellbeing and that all cultures are of equal value.[9] Patrick West, author of *The Poverty of Multiculturalism*, raises some similar criticisms. He condemns multiculturalism as a policy that has served only to 'divide the population into groupsicles of competing ethnicities'.[10] He does not endorse the mantra that all cultures are equal and that museums, as well as other areas, should be used as a means to celebrate difference and he even argues that state-sponsored multiculturalism has been counter-productive and worsens race relations. For West one of the greatest offences is the promotion of cultural relativism, the belief that no culture is better than another and that we should actively promote difference, which he argues has led in the UK to a reluctance to celebrate British and Christian cultures in comparison with some others.[11] For Kenan Malik, who encourages the distinction between multiculturalism as a lived experience and as an ideology, promotion of the latter is 'politically dangerous' and likely to undermine the former.[12] For Malik the promotion of cultural pluralism, through multiculturalism, has not been a means to establish equality, but rather 'an accommodation to the persistence of inequality', and differences are rationalised 'not as the negative product of racism or discrimination but the positive result of multiculturalism'.[13]

Indeed, certain statements in the various museum-based cultural diversity policies from around the world would cause such critics to stand up in protest. Both the UNESCO and the ICOM statements quoted above emphasise the importance of acknowledging all cultures and that this is a human right. Barry and West both criticise the assertion that all culture is equally valid, challenging it with examples of customs that are non-peaceful, abusive and sometimes dangerous. West is of the opinion that a policy agenda singling out minority groups for particular attention leads to tension, and will erode the richness of culture. Malik argues that nurturing difference allows fewer opportunities for cultures to learn from each other so as to enrich experiences of multiculturalism. Anthropologists have argued for less acceptance of the absolute nature of legal and ethical arguments drawn from the human rights context. For them human rights is a socially constructed phenomenon, largely originating from western society.[14] Marie-Bénédicte Dembour, for instance, objects to the belief in definite universal human rights and presents human rights as serving to 'articulate political claims in a way that clothes them with an aura of incontestable legitimacy'.[15] Furthermore, Mary Ann Glendon criticises the 'rapidly expanding catalog of rights' that not only 'multiplies the occasions for collisions, but risks trivialising core democratic values', which in its simplistic and absolute form can ignore social costs and rights of others.[16]

In a debate hosted by *Spiked*, an online publication, some key professionals in the UK sector provided their experiences and opinions regarding the links that have been made between culture and diversity policy. Deirdre Figueiredo draws attention to 'institutional racism' in our cultural institutions, the lack of diversity within the senior levels, and the well-established infrastructure that privileges particular approaches to culture. She favours cultural diversity policy as a means to target resources, challenge assumptions, build capacity and shift the balance of power, because otherwise such a shift would happen at a 'tortoise pace'.[17] In a commissioned response, Naseem Khan, who has been responsible for forwarding the cultural diversity agenda in the Arts Council of England, argues that cultural diversity policy has been a means to expose the barriers within the structures of the arts.[18] In her 2002 report to the Arts Council Khan states that the need for such policies emerged from structures that 'marginalised groups and individuals'. She praises the achievements of initiatives such as the Arts Council New Audiences Programmes, which targeted funding for partnerships between mainstream institutions and community-based cultural groups.[19]

Speaking at the same debate, but against cultural diversity policy, Jatinder Verma argued that such policy has led to an institutionalisation of ethnicity, which forgets the 'ever-present' nature of ethnicity in British arts, and leads to increased marginalisation.[20] For Tony Graves, this has brought about a 'box-ticking' culture wherein cultural policy is reduced to statistics and audit trails.[21] For Tiffany Jenkins, the obligation to develop cultural diversity policy is 'an extension of political interference in the arts', which will lead to a failure to judge arts by aesthetic groups and an indifference to minority arts.[22] What seems to have escaped Jenkins is the point made by Khan: 'it is a mistake to divorce the arts from the political and social conditions'.[23] Although Jenkins is drawing attention to direct political intervention, and Khan is referring to the political and social context, the politics of social policy is shaped by and shapes the politics of the social situation. The microanalysis of individual initiatives and policy recommendations may cause us to overlook the larger context that shapes value and values. So although tokenism, pigeon-holing and failing to nurture the best of the arts is inappropriate, we should perhaps, as Anna Somers Cocks recommends, look beyond the 'integrations of minorities into the world of the majority' and encourage the majority to embrace 'the world of the minority'.[24] Maybe by doing so we can achieve much less of a binary of minority/majority and instead create a broader understanding of valued culture.

Cultural diversity in relation to museum policy and practice

The arguments that have been put forward by the museum sector that justify the adoption of cultural diversity approaches have been well summarised by Lola Young.[25] Writing for the Museum of London, Young bases her support for embracing cultural diversity policy on four areas. She begins by saying that museums need to embrace the legal obligations to promote equality and end discrimination. She follows this with the argument that on intellectual grounds museums must engage with a breadth of issues to reflect contemporary society properly. This, she believes, is underpinned by the ethical case, which relates cultural diversity to human rights and social justice. Finally she adopts the business case that should make museums wish to maximise their audiences and public support. These motivations sustain many of the examples of how museums have engaged with multiculturalism and cultural diversity, and they have had a profound influence on museum practice.

National museum bodies in the UK, Australia, South Africa and the US, to name but a few, have each produced policy guidance on cultural diversity. The Cultural Diversity Policy adopted by Museum Australia focuses on the idea of rights; the policy declares that all Australians have the right to see elements of their culture preserved and interpreted in museums. This, the policy advocates, should impact on collections development, public programmes, access, staffing and human resources, and governance of the museum. In the Australian example, it is not only museum collections, staff and programming that should reflect diversity; museums are also asked to take a proactive role in shaping attitudes to cultural diversity and have been asked to 'promote understanding, acceptance and tolerance of cultural difference'.[26] Again, museums are being allocated an ethical role and are being thought of as places that can explore modern concerns such as human rights.

In the UK, museum services across England have issued diversity statements that have responded to various local needs. In practice, many museums have staff, often in the learning or outreach sections, responsible for developing links and running initiatives related to cultural diversity priorities. In 2000 the UK Museums and Galleries Commission produced a Fact Sheet, written by Naseem Khan, on cultural diversity, encouraging museums to rethink their collecting policy and the display and interpretation of collections. They also asked that greater consideration be given to staffing, use of minority languages in displays and more consistent links between the museum and minority groups. The result, they hope, 'is a museum, which demonstrates its relevance to its community and wider society'.[27] Within this document the concern for cultural diversity is motivated by both social and pragmatic concerns. Museums are described as having a 'vital part to play in presenting an inclusive vision of society'; as public institutions they need to 'find ways to communicate with a wider public'; and, using rationale, 'economics argue forcibly for the wisdom of maximising attendance through expanding the range of visitors'.[28] So, if a concern for the good of society is not convincing enough, increasing visitor numbers to the museum might persuade.

In general, the support for embracing multiculturalism in museums is an interest in increasing relevance of museums to a greater range of audiences and illustrating commitment to exploring issues that are more socially relevant. Later Re:source, the Council for Museums, Archives and Libraries, supported the formation of regional networks throughout Britain that would address cultural diversity within the sector and develop diversity policies for museums. The early years of the North West Cultural Diversity Network, for instance, saw the hosting of seminars to look at the implications of the diversity agenda for the area. The network published a research project identifying understanding of cultural diversity and addressed practical issues for museums, libraries and archives in working with diverse audiences. An online regional project directory has been used to summarise projects relating to cultural diversity and to provide a support and ideas network. The North West Cultural Diversity Network has also increased funding for audience development work. One such project was the development of a cultural diversity collecting strategy in the Rochdale area with the aim to increase the representation of South Asian communities in local collections.[29] In such cases these policies and museum initiatives are seeking for museums to reflect better the diversity of the society within which they are situated. A museum that has embraced its responsibilities for cultural diversity should have this reflected in the collections they hold and display, the stories they tell, audiences they attract and people the museums employ.

Diversify: Museums Association, UK

This thinking has shaped the entirety of museum practice. Since 1998 the UK Museums Association has used positive action as a means to encourage people from under-represented minorities to take up posts in the museum sector. Their goal is to increase workforce diversity: they argue that 7 per cent of the UK workforce is of Asian, African Caribbean or Chinese descent yet only 2 per cent of the museum workforce is from these minority groups. The Museums Association works with universities and museums, offering traineeships and bursaries, to enable people from ethnic minorities to gain the skills to enter museums and move into middle and senior management.[30] A report on the impact of the traineeships, written by Gaby Porter for the Museums, Libraries and Archives Council, found that trainees were unanimous that these opportunities were a positive experience and museums participating in the scheme felt they had benefited. The scheme is promoted on the basis of positive action, which is an idea drawn from the 1976 Race Relations Act (section 38) that allows for the provision of 'discriminatory training'. The Act renders lawful, under certain conditions, the provision and promotion of facilities and training opportunities that focus only on people from ethnic minorities.[31] 'Positive Action', the term that replaces 'discriminatory training' in the workplace, has become an approved method of overcoming 'the accumulated effects of past discrimination'.[32] Despite its increasing acceptance, several of the participants in the Diversify Initiative, interviewed by Porter, voiced their discomfort with the idea of positive action. One participant commented that she felt uncomfortable that her involvement was 'on the basis of my colour'. Others felt the existence of the scheme was a 'touchy subject' and sensed resistance from those who felt she was 'jumping the queue'. Another commented she was always introduced as the 'positive action trainee', as if to say 'aren't we good, we've got one'.[33] These comments from participants reveal the issues some have with activity that seems to favour one group over another, even if it is based on readdressing past injustice or attempts to create a more equal representation. It is similar to the criticism that is rendered at action that deliberately tries to increase opportunities for women in politics or the workplace. Increasing acceptability is often a case of revealing the context within which such policies are being developed and the range of benefits their success will introduce.

Reassessing What We Collect, Museum of London

As well as staffing, the question of how representative museum collections are of their local and national communities has been receiving greater attention. This was one of the key motivations underpinning the Reassessing What We Collect project at the Museum of London.[34] Initiated in 2004, the primary purpose of the project is to link with many communities in London, including African, Asian, Caribbean and North American as well as Disabled London, and the Lesbian, Gay, Bisexual and Transgendered communities. The project encourages curatorial staff to look again at their museum collections and to reorder them into an online database sorted according to London communities (as defined by the 2001 UK population census). The online resource is searchable by community name, and object images and descriptions are linked to those communities. From a potential of one million items in its collection, in August 2006 the database listed approximately 300 objects that can be linked to particular communities. Through new acquisitions, donations and better awareness of current collections, in the next two years the Museum hopes to add another thousand objects to that database.[35]

To me it seems quite reasonable that in a world of so many cultures, and in societies of mixed histories, faiths and practices, this variation should be represented in museums. With regard to the Museum of London, in a collection of over a million objects telling the history of London from prehistory to the present day it seems a shame that only 300 objects, and later maybe only a thousand more, will be linked to the culturally diverse communities of that city. One could argue that the entire collection reflects the stories of London as capital of Britain, as part of the British Empire, and as linked to cultures and countries around the world. There is a risk that targeting of specific objects, and linking them to particular groups, may reduce appreciation of the range of people to whom objects are relevant. Such categorisation may limit our thinking about objects, their meanings and their potentials. It could serve further to pigeonhole or generalise about culture and its complexity. Moreover, it might curb how we think about our own identity and what objects we consider significant to ourselves. In its favour, however, the project should be welcomed as an opportunity for the Museum of London to rethink its entire collections, working practices and exhibitions. It may challenge people who don't believe the Museum has objects of relevance to them and encourage people to explore links with the Museum. This is the perspective taken by Raminder Kaur, in his essay for the Reassessing What We Collect project, in which he considered the Museum's current collections with regard to ethnicity/race, sexuality and disability. He argued that the appreciation of difference, and 'difference within difference',[36] is something that should pervade every aspect of museum practice. He suggested that the broader interpretation of existing collections, triggered by this initiative, should enhance the appeal of the Museum to both regular and new audiences.

Our People Our Times, Northern Ireland Museums Council

Exhibition development has also been influenced by the greater profile of policy in the areas of multiculturalism and cultural diversity. The exhibition Our People Our Times, created by the Northern Ireland Museums Council and later added to by local museums, is one such example (Fig. 5.1). The exhibition was developed in 2004 and is one of a number of exhibitions devised by the NIMC since its foundation in the early 1990s. Other exhibitions include examples which explored local identities and others focusing on aspects of social history. In every case NIMC provides a spinal exhibition of key panels, which then tours local museums. Those museums are encouraged to work with local people and

Figure 5.1 Our People Our Times exhibition, Workhouse Museum, Londonderry

communities to add panels, collections and workshops applicable to their own areas. This has been a means for NIMC to support the sector in the development of new exhibitions and, sometimes, to explore subject areas that they may otherwise avoid. This was the case with the development of Our People Our Times. Chris Bailey, Director of Northern Ireland Museums Council, found that initially some museum staff could not see the value of an exhibition on the subject of migration into Northern Ireland. Since its creation, however, he has been pleased with the positive response from the sector and achievements of particular museums.[37] Focusing on the experience of migration into Northern Ireland, the exhibition is described as 'a history of Northern Ireland's cultural diversity'. It begins in the Mesolithic period with 'Ireland's first migrants' and continues by telling the story of arrivals in the archaeological and historical periods. Communities more often thought to be part of recent arrivals, such as travellers, Jewish communities and Italians, are shown to have been in Northern Ireland since the eighteenth and nineteenth centuries. Others such as the Indian community have been in Northern Ireland since the 1930s, and the Chinese community since the 1960s. Both these groups, and individuals who have arrived more recently, are celebrated for their contributions to medicine, the arts, food and manufacturing.

In the Foreword to the accompanying exhibition booklet the Chief Executive of the Community Relations Council, Duncan Morrow, writes that the exhibition is a means to emphasise that Northern Ireland has always been a changing place and to accept that diversity is something we should 'earnestly wish for, not a disaster to be resisted'.[38] The NIMC Chairman wants to remind us that 'we are all "diverse" – whether our ancestors came here hundreds of years ago, or we have just recently arrived'.[39] In Northern Ireland, where difference has been a sectarian issue and recent arrivals have been subject to racist violence, these are important lessons. Coverage of the exhibition in a local paper in County Fermanagh, under the title 'Welcoming Diversity', opened with reference to recent attacks in the county – the museum is described as 'working to make amends' by exhibiting the 'treasures' brought by immigrants and giving them an opportunity to 'share their culture with their neighbours'.[40] Speaking about the development and success of the exhibition, Development Officer Bronagh Cleary was saddened by the racist events and hoped the exhibition provided a positive experience both for vulnerable communities and for those needing to learn more about the diverse communities now found in the county.[41] In preparation for hosting the exhibition Fermanagh County Museum involved staff from education, curatorial and marketing areas, so as to get a balance of activities and approaches. They worked with Women of the World, a local community group with whom they already had a good relationship, and forged links with the Migrant Information Education Unit (MiE-U), a local group set up to assist recent arrivals to the county, mostly from Eastern Europe. The resulting exhibition included objects from the Philippines, Morocco, Chile, Hong Kong, Lithuania and Poland. Special events included food tastings, dance workshops, arts and crafts, music and storytelling. These were used to celebrate aspects of Irish and Ulster-Scots culture as well as those originating from further afield.

For the Fermanagh County Museum one of the strengths of the exhibition was the opportunity it provided for people to meet each other, both those from different migrant communities and others with longer links with the county. It also provided the museum with an opportunity to develop more meaningful links with community groups. For instance, the Development Officer found the Migrant Information Education Unit initially very cautious of a potential link with the museum – feeling that their members were in Northern Ireland for employment reasons and not as cultural representatives. However, once the museum met with members, and objectives were discussed, involvement between MiE-U and the museum was very positive and plans are underway to continue the link through further museum-based initiatives.

Representation of the San community in the South African Museum

The examples of the Diversify scheme, the Reassessing What We Collect project, and the Our People Our Times exhibition are each concerned with the idea of representation. Charles Taylor, an advocate of multiculturalism, conceptualises the idea as a concern for recognition, claiming that recognition is essential for the construction of our identity and misrecognition can cause people to suffer damage and distortion.[42] For Taylor due recognition is a 'vital human need'.[43] This, he argues, is because identity is 'socially derived' and formed as a result of dialogue with others – the nature of that dialogue will produce positive or negative senses of self and esteem. So, to encourage a positive sense of self, he endorses the politics of equal respect: 'that we all recognize the equal value of different cultures; that we not only let them survive, but acknowledge their *worth*' (original emphasis).[44] It is this idea of acknowledgement that relates to the work of the museum sector. Museums are often cited as places that can provide recognition of worth. Whether or not a group is represented in museum collections and displays, and the nature of that interpretation, can be used as an indicator of how that group is valued and the role it plays in contemporary society. There are many examples of inclusion in a museum display as bringing pride and recognition to a person or community; when the situation is reversed, exclusion is often read as an indication that a particular group, its history and its culture are of little value.

In Cape Town the museum sector is attempting to reverse a legacy of exclusion and misrepresentation of black South Africans that included the neglect of their history; avoidance of certain periods of history, such as slavery; and the exclusion of black history from the categories of cultural history and art. Still today there is a lack of black people represented in middle and high management in South Africa's museums. In relation to the latter, the reversal of this situation was one of the motivations underpinning the establishment of the Robben Island Training Programme in museum and heritage studies in the mid-1990s. Now well established, the programme is supported by Affirmative Action bursaries,[45] which have been designed to ensure designated groups (black people, women and people with disabilities) have equal opportunities in the workplace.[46]

The segregation of ideas and people, found in established museums in Cape Town, is most striking in the displays of the South African Cultural History Museum (SACHM) and the South African Museum (SAM). The SACHM, which was formed in 1965, mainly focuses on Greek and Egyptian antiquities; European costume, silver and furniture; and Japanese ceramics and costume. The South African Museum is principally a natural history and anthropology museum. The decision to represent the history of African people amongst natural history rather than cultural history has been interpreted as an expression of apartheid – of the belief that high cultural attainment is of European origin whereas black history is undeveloped. Since the end of apartheid both the SAM and the SACHM have worked at readdressing their displays. The difficulties involved in achieving successful museum representation are demonstrated by the recent attempts to redevelop the South African Galleries in the SAM. In 2001 a controversial diorama, composed of life-casts of indigenous people, was removed from display. The SAM saw the closing of the diorama as 'a symbolic reminder of the transformation of our museum to a more democratic institution'. However, for many years this was considered one of the most popular exhibitions in the museum. The root of the difficulties with the display lies with its origins. In 1906 the then Director of the SAM initiated a project to make life-casts of 'aboriginals of the Bush and Hottentot races', then thought to be near extinction.[47] This was part of a project that was interested in the question of racial origins and the Director asked that models be taken from the 'living flesh' of survivors of these nearly extinguished races. Prisons were thought to be one such source, and in 1907 the Superintendent of the Convict Station in Kimberley replied to say that he had some 'fairly good specimens of their race'; he also added, 'I might point out that it is most difficult nowadays to find a pure-blooded specimen'.[48] Some of the selection criteria were based on genital features. People were then photographed naked, and measured in minute detail, and a selected number were cast. In her review of the practice Patricia Davison wrote that the people became 'dehumanized to objects of study' and it is quite likely those in convict stations were not given the right to refuse.[49] When first put on public display in the early twentieth century the people who were cast were used to tell the story of racial type, with no reference to social or cultural context; they were 'literally objectivized and reduced to scientific specimens'.[50] More recently, and recognising this point, the museum attempted to engage visitors with the tensions associated with the exhibit. It provided an explanation of the socio-political context of the diorama and presented questions that encouraged visitors to critique the museum.

The diorama that was removed from the SAM in 2001 was created in the 1960s and composed of these original casts. At the time of its removal the Chief Executive Officer of the Iziko Museums of Cape Town stated that the diorama was being closed because 'it represents a time when Bushmen were treated like specimens in a natural history museum . . . closing it is a symbol that our museums are changing'. He also spoke of it being the product of a form of museum practice that was now defunct.[51] For the museum, this was an important act of planning for the future and creating more democratic processes based on consultation with stakeholder communities and revisiting the interpretations of history and culture. The SAM saw the diorama as a form of misrepresentation of indigenous communities and on TV news coverage at the time San leaders referred to the display as making them appear 'barbaric' and as being a 'thorn in their side'.[52] However, other San representatives quoted in newspaper coverage referred to the loss of the diorama as meaning their history was being removed from the museum. In an article titled 'San shocked at closure of exhibit' San community groups are quoted as saying that there is so little representation of them in museums that this exhibition must remain – one stated, 'we have lost a lot of our history. That exhibition must stay'. Others stated that they would like the display to be remounted in a San Cultural Centre, or redisplayed as a means to show how San people have been treated by museums.[53] The diorama was one of the most popular exhibits in the museum – in 2006, five years after it was removed, the future of the diorama is still being discussed.

Cultural diversity and museum change

The case of the representation of the San people in the South African Museum, and the differing responses to the diorama, some in favour and some against, is an example of how difficult it is to balance different understandings of interpretation and representation in museum space. Public display adds resonance, impact and meaning to the stories being told in exhibition spaces. Inclusion and exclusion from display, and the nature of those processes, have meaning and consequences. Those meanings will be interpreted differently according to the position of the person doing the interpretation. On occasion, when the stakes are high, this will lead to tension and conflict. In relation to museums and heritage these tensions most often relate to how the display relates to our sense of identity. This is in respect to both how we ourselves are being represented and how we understand, value and represent the identity of others. In the issues of museum practice provided above, examples of staffing, collecting and the creation of exhibitions have each attempted to revisit established museum practice with new ideas of how best to represent changing and diverse identities. Each of the initiatives has attempted to take account of aspects of best practice in relation to multiculturalism and cultural diversity policy. As a result, it appears that the museum as an institution is changing because of greater awareness of new communities.

There is no doubt that the rise of interest in embracing cultural diversity and multiculturalism policy has increased the pace of changes in museum practice – interest in new forms of collecting, new histories on display and new ways of communicating. What is more difficult to assess is how deeply founded these changes are. Are they taking place at the core or are they simply at the periphery? Are they long-term changes or short-term reactions? Are they by the concern of the majority in the museum sector, or only a few? The responses to these questions depend on the institution itself and the time at which the question is being asked. In some cases changes are taking place at the core, and the intention is to make long-term changes and develop commitment across the museum. This may be the situation for a number of years, and emphasis may later shift. In other cases, critics have argued that attempts to adopt the diversity agenda, although appearing to connect with racial and cultural minorities, have sometimes failed to do so. Roshi Naidoo has argued that this may arise from a poor understanding of those minority groups, their experiences and their histories, and an inability to recognise or shed traditional prejudices. In such cases, she believes that well-intentioned 'liberal agendas' can have little impact.[54] Greater self-awareness and a willingness to invite those outside the museum to participate in evaluation of new programmes could well be a means to lessen this danger.

6

Museums and community relations in Northern Ireland

In Northern Ireland the promotion of good community relations over the past three decades has almost become an industry in itself, which, in that period, has shifted in character and emphasis. From the point of view of relations, this has been a shift in concern for the 'two communities' of Northern Ireland (labelled as Protestant and Catholic; unionist and nationalist; or loyalist and republican) to a broader desire to increase understanding of diverse communities, including those of different religious, ethnic, political or gender backgrounds. Community relations strategies have been subject to a critique similar to that raised against some forms of cultural diversity and multiculturalism policy, with regard to both the wisdom of state-led strategies and the involvement of museums. In relation to the community relations agenda the role of museums has also changed over the past thirty years, with museums at first presenting themselves as 'oases of calm', where the Troubles did not intrude, to more recently engaging in the 'good relations' initiatives, which link to recent Government policy emerging from Northern Ireland.

The promotion of understanding, appreciation and acceptance of difference, which have been discussed in the previous chapter, take on additional meanings and roles when brought to a political and cultural context like Northern Ireland. Here they have been merged with the idea and practice of community relations and regarded as able to make a contribution to resolving the conflict. Adding to the complexity, responses to the agendas of multiculturalism are often linked to the politics of state and community. The Northern Ireland situation emphasises the political nature of these concepts and allows us to interrogate the ideas, and their application in museums, even further.

This chapter begins by exploring ideas of community relations as adopted in Northern Ireland and how they have shifted with time. What these changes mean for how we understand community relations is emphasised. The second and third sections look to the links that have been made between community relations and museums: both through the general association as a form of educational practice and specifically through the development of a museum in a city that has endured some of the worst experiences of the Troubles. The chapter finishes with a consideration of the current interest in linking museums with the idea of 'good relations', a concept that has revisited the traditional idea of community relations.

The ideas of community relations in Northern Ireland

Although many places have social problems that can be related to issues of race, identity and belonging, in Northern Ireland these problems have been acute over a sustained period of time. The conflict or 'Troubles'[1] experienced in Northern Ireland since the late 1960s have often been interpreted as relating to issues of representation, as well as to political and cultural relations between the rest of the United Kingdom and the Republic of Ireland. In addition the human cost has been substantial. The *Cost of the Troubles* study, published in 1999, calculated that between 1969 and the 1994 ceasefire 3585 people were killed in the Troubles, almost half of whom were civilians, and over 40,000 people injured. In addition, the Troubles have also been shown to have led to high levels of deprivation as well as emotional and physical distress.[2] Most recently, the impact of racism directed at new communities in Northern Ireland has caused increased concern.

During the period of the Troubles, and since, community relations work has received a higher profile as a means to tackle the attitudes and beliefs that have sustained prejudice and division in Northern Ireland. Its chief aim has been to improve understanding between what has been traditionally regarded as the two communities in Northern Ireland (unionist/nationalist, loyalist/republican or Protestant/Catholic). This has been promoted by the state through the Central Community Relations Unit, in local government by the District Council Community Relations Programme and on the ground by local community activists. It has also become an important part of the work of the education sector, through the Education for Mutual Understanding (EMU) and Cultural Heritage initiatives. In 2005 the Office of the First Minister and Deputy First Minister introduced a 'good relations' strategy and policy, which is to be integrated with all aspects of public life, including education, the workplace and at community level.

Hughes and Donnelly, in their review of how community relations work has been supported and developed by governing bodies in Northern Ireland, have distilled the shifting approaches into distinct phases. In the early 1980s it was one that encouraged greater cross-community contact, mutual understanding and respect for different cultures and traditions. This was fostered through the Central Community Relations Unit and new education programmes. Later, emphasis was placed on the causes of conflict, such as disadvantage and discrimination, rather than on the symptoms, such as high levels of segregation and division. This is demonstrated by the introduction of fair employment legislation and policy initiatives to target social need. Since the late 1990s emphasis has been on the promotion of cultural, religious and political pluralism as well as the equality agenda.[3] More recently, community relations work has been twinned with the notion of cultural diversity, and it operates on the basis of key principles such as respect for diversity, recognition of interdependence of different interest or identity groupings, and equality of access.[4] As well as the shift in the nature of community relations work in Northern Ireland, there has also been a change in how certain policy agendas have been interpreted. This is demonstrated by the approach to cultural diversity since its rise in the 1970s to its current form in the late 1990s and early 2000s. This shift has been described as a move from the old pluralist agenda, formed to address conflicts between the two communities in Northern Ireland, to a new pluralist agenda that takes broader issues into account.[5] The arrival of immigrants in Northern Ireland, and associated race-related issues, has urged us to move away from the already outdated two-community approach and to consider our own issues in the context of representation, language, work and living experiences for these new populations.

In addition to this state-led approach there have been many community-based peace initiatives led by local groups and leaders, often within their own Protestant or Catholic communities and sometimes with a cross-community dimension. Community relations work in Northern Ireland is an area that people do not enter lightly. Often personal experiences motivate people to engage in such activity, and individual passions and commitment drive their work. The community relations officer at the Ulster Folk and Transport Museum, for instance, has been undertaking such work in a private capacity for at least as long as she has in the museum. She is deeply committed to this area of work, believing that for many it has 'freed them from their prejudices'.[6] As a result of working with the same young people over a number of years, she has seen changing attitudes and improved relations. For her there is no disputing the positive impact of community relations work as supported and developed by the Community Relations Council and similar bodies in Northern Ireland.[7]

Approaches to community relations work in Northern Ireland, and moves into the areas of multiculturalism and cultural diversity policies, have been the subject of some criticism. At the core of the debate are the different approaches that are each a consequence of state and non-state relations, political goals and agendas. Researcher and activist Robbie McVeigh argues that the politics of community development and community relations are intertwined with the politics of Northern Ireland. He sees state-led community relations in Northern Ireland as a means to 'manage' the conflict with a 'blandness' that is counter-productive and fails to challenge the system within which it is situated.[8] Bill Rolston, considering the adoption of a multiculturalism discourse in Northern Ireland, believes it has been used to manage sectarian divisions and provide simplistic acceptance for the 'two traditions' by ignoring power structures.[9] For him, the multiculturalism agenda has depoliticised history, has reduced it to relativism, and has been a form of social engineering aiming to replace the political problem with an acceptable idea of culture.

The contribution of the museum sector in Northern Ireland

This debate concerning community relations in Northern Ireland provides a hint at the difficulties facing the museum sector if it wishes to engage with the recent history of Northern Ireland in its displays or to get involved in community relations work. The act of interpretation and presentation of the past carries a certain amount of risk: interpretations can be accused of misrepresentation, over-simplification or neglect. In addition, as shown, through the very involvement with community relations approaches and agendas, led by Government, the sector could be accused of legitimising and furthering a system that aims to pacify and maintain the status quo. Within this context it is not surprising that many museums have often shied away from commenting on the Troubles in their displays. As a result, community relations work of museums is a fairly recent initiative, stemming from the rise of this area within government and education sectors.

At the height of the Troubles, museums were regarded as one of the places that ought to represent 'an oasis of calm'. This notion, developed in relation to schools, was described by Anthony Buckley, a curator at Ulster Folk and Transport Museum: 'when homes were being nightly raided, when rioting was an everyday occurrence, and when explosions and gunfire regularly rattled the windows, one could walk into a school and find peace'.[10] In this context museums were to be neutral territory, where the Troubles would not intrude. According to Buckley, this was achieved by the 'physical exclusion of "the men of violence" ' and keeping out of the museum gallery 'contentious forms of debate that could "politicise" these places'.[11] Later this began to change, with increased support for exhibitions and posts exploring culture and identity issues relating to the Troubles. In the 1990s the European Union's Special Support Programme for Peace and Reconciliation funded the post of Outreach Officer at the Ulster Museum to work on such areas. The post was closely associated with the Community Relations Council: the Council administered its funding and monitored activity through regular reports. The outreach activity has taken the form of working on exhibitions exploring identity in Northern Ireland, workshops with adults based around the development of a CD-ROM on the Troubles, and adult community history projects based in areas that have had high rates of violence or polarisation as a result of the Troubles. Through this post, the museum made a number of links with cross-community and single-interest groups in Northern Ireland.[12] Building upon this area, the Ulster Museum has mounted a number of temporary exhibitions that explore identity and the Troubles, such as Icons of Identity in October 2000 to April 2001 (Figure 6.1) and Conflict: The Irish at War (Figure 6.2) in December 2003 to August 2006.

As well as the national museums, a number of local museums across Northern Ireland now have specific programmes that tie in with the community relations component of the school curriculum. The Community Education Officer in Down County Museum, for instance, has developed a programme focused on developing a sense of community identity and civic pride, and an appreciation of the diversity of cultural traditions. Museum staff believe they have created a

Figure 6.1 Icons of Identity exhibition, Ulster Museum

shared and safe museum space.[13] The museum has attempted to broaden its audience through a diverse range of activities, such as lectures, living history events, mock trails and drama, focusing on historical events that previously may have been avoided because of their controversial nature.[14]

It can be said that, in the most part, the museum sector has become involved with direct community relations activity as a result of the demand emerging from elsewhere, most prominently the schools community relations programmes. Since the 1980s the Department of Education for Northern Ireland (DENI) has encouraged the development of education programmes that aim to promote better community relations.[15] In 1992, as a result of the Education Reform (Northern Ireland) Order of 1989, the themes of Education for Mutual Under-standing (EMU) and Cultural Heritage (CH) became a compulsory part of the Northern Ireland school curriculum. Its purpose was to enable students to learn respect for themselves and others and to appreciate interdependence of people in

Figure 6.2 Conflict exhibition, Ulster Museum

society. The initiative also encouraged participants to develop a better under-standing of differing cultural traditions and to appreciate how conflict may be handled in non-violent ways.[16] Since that date EMU and CH have been an important part of the Schools Community Relations Programme, whose remit is to bring together children from Protestant and Catholic schools to participate in community relations programmes. Museums in Northern Ireland have developed education materials to support EMU and CH and this has been regarded as an opportunity for museums to become, in the words of a former museum director, centres to 'enhance mutual respect for varying cultural tradi-tions' and a neutral space where social discovery is 'safe'.[17] The Department of Education has supported the provision of EMU-related facilities in the national museums in Northern Ireland that it believes 'recreate the historical dimension in a non-threatening manner and in which groups can share the exploration of their past'.[18] Education Officers generally see museums as able to use collections and expertise as a means to support the work of teachers and, possibly, explore new areas. In return teachers have welcomed community relations workshops in museums as an opportunity for them to be learners alongside the pupils and empower them with confidence for future work.[19] As museum staff have become more expert in community relations work, through participation in various training programmes in that area, they have received greater support from schools. Teacher feedback has shown appreciation for the provision of resources in an area they often feel ill equipped to deal with in the classroom.[20]

More recently, the earlier EMU schemes have evolved into widespread community relations programmes that are to filter through entire school planning and are to become focused less directly on the Troubles and more on understanding difference. The Department of Education in Northern Ireland is currently investing £3.4 million per annum to promote community relations in formal and informal education. A Schools Community Relations Programme has been devised, administered by local Education and Library Boards, whose chief aim is to 'develop an awareness and understanding of religious, cultural and political diversity within our society'.[21] Guided by the Community Relations Support Panel, which has produced extensive resources for teachers in schools, this new community relations curriculum has the aim to 'empower young people' to make 'informed and responsible choices throughout their lives', which it is hoped will lead to a more peaceful society. It focuses on personal and mutual understanding, moral character, citizenship and cultural understanding (see Table 6.1),[22]

Table 6.1 Developing community relations practice: Northern Ireland school curriculum

---

The learning opportunities provided through the Northern Ireland Curriculum should help young people to:

Personal and Mutual Understanding
- develop self-confidence, self discipline and self-esteem
- understand their own and others' feelings and emotions
- listen to and interact positively with others
- explore and understand how others live

Moral Character
- understand that values, choices and decisions should be informed by a sense of fairness
- take responsibility for their actions
- develop tolerance and mutual respect for others

Citizenship
- become aware of some of their rights and responsibilities
- become aware of some of the issues and problems in society
- contribute to creating a better world for those around them

Cultural Understanding
- understand some of their own and others' cultural traditions
- be aware of how we rely on each other

---

and teachers are asked to build this into their school programmes and activities. Museums have responded to the new emphasis through the development of programmes directly linked to the above aims and objectives and by shifting the emphasis of museum posts that now, for instance, give greater attention to the idea of citizenship.

Community relations work at the Ulster Folk and Transport Museum

Approximately 30,000 children a year take part in the community relations programmes developed by the Education Department at the Ulster Folk and Transport Museum (UFTM). The current programmes are the result of over fifteen years of the museum engaging with issues such as identity, tolerance, prejudice and shared cultural heritage. In the present climate, the UFTM Education Department aims to contribute to providing children with the skills to 'live in a multicultural society and use history as a way of learning from the past to live in the future'.[23] For now, the museum offers a series of seven workshops that have been developed according to the staff expertise and that tie in with the Northern Ireland schools curriculum (see Table 6.1). The programmes range from a 'First Contact' session, based on interactive games to assist students from different backgrounds to get to know each other, to those that encourage students to think about the different sides to stories or events, to discuss the formation of identity and the construction of culture, and to compare and contrast the use of symbols. Other programmes consider the concept of prejudice and resolving conflict amongst peers. The UFTM feels that it has responded to these goals with a programme that has as its core values 'equity, diversity and inter-dependence' and that encourages students to 'explore their own and each other's identity, heritage and culture'.[24] These values, which underpin the museum programme, have been devised in consultation with teachers. Furthermore, the programmes are subject to constant evaluation and have been reworked over the years according to feedback and as staff gain more experience in the area. The museum encourages schools from different backgrounds, which are coming together on a visit, to meet with each other, create shared objectives, and work with the museum to tailor a visit that best suits the needs of the school and the children. The museum arranges planning days prior to school visits and has had representation at a parents' evening at a local school to answer questions about the community relations programme at the museum in order to alleviate any fears parents may have.[25]

The programmes are devised to link in with the collections and buildings on display at the museum, such as the Protestant and Catholic churches, an Orange Hall,[26] a police station, a court house, and houses for the clergy. A programme for Key Stage 2 and Key Stage 3, for instance, is based on a true story of a couple in a mixed marriage whose house is now part of the museum collection and whose love 'triumphed over sectarianism and cultural differences'.[27] The workshop encourages students to discuss aspects of the life of a Protestant and Catholic couple such as sectarian attitudes, accepting diversity and living with differences. They discuss experiences the couple may have had: problems arising from being of different faiths, having different first languages, the families' reactions to their relationship, their choice of church in which to get married, and sacrifices each had to make by marrying someone of a different faith. The students are encouraged to consider how to overcome difference, the nature of compromise and how these issues may apply to their own lives.[28] Student feedback from a group of 9–11 year olds indicated a greater awareness of other people's lives and religions – one child observing correctly that 'William church had no Jesus on the cross, Winnie church had a Jesus on the cross'.[29] In the evaluation after the programme the students are asked if they think they will remember what they have talked about during that day and whether they will try and do anything differently now (see responses in Table 6.2).[30]

The museum follows up its evaluation feedback from pupils and teachers with a report that it sends to the schools involved. Within the report they summarise the main findings and make recommendations for future work that the schools might engage in, either amongst themselves or as a further link with the museum. In one such report, sent out after a joint visit of a predominantly Catholic and a predominantly Protestant secondary school, the Education Department was able to comment on the students' willingness to learn about other identities, many noting they would like to find out more about the identity with which they do not normally identify. When asked what they felt they had learnt on the visit, approximately three-quarters of a group of forty students stated 'to respect others', with many citing greater tolerance, cultural awareness, and thinking about sameness rather than difference, as well as learning to be 'nicer'.[31]

Table 6.2 Sample of feedback from students and teachers attending UFTM community relations workshops

Students
'I will believe that just because people are catholics they are just like us'
'It makes me think different'
'I would not fight with catholics'
'I hope that everybody understands each other we will have no fighting'
'I will be fair to the protestants'
'I'm going to stick up for people who have catholic and protestant parents'

Teachers
'The children became relaxed with ourselves and each other – ready to engage with discussion and groupwork'
'The discussion was clearly focused on identity and prejudice and the children easily and readily absorbed the information'
'Very good at getting the message of working together and appreciating differences'
'I felt that if the children had raised any difficult issues they would have been dealt with and discussed safely'

The development of a museum in a troubled city

The Tower Museum in Derry/Londonderry, a city in which the political divide of Northern Ireland is expressed in its dual names, has been notable in the region for being the only publicly funded museum to consider the history of the Troubles in its permanent galleries. The museum is located in a city that has experienced some of the worst events of the Troubles and the highest proportion of Troubles-related deaths.[32] In addition, significant areas of the city are ranked amongst the most deprived parts of Northern Ireland.[33]

Until the early 1990s Derry was without a municipal museum. A local museum had existed for a while in the early twentieth century and since the 1970s the City Council had been cultivating cultural activity. The key for the establishment of the Tower Museum was the activity of the Inner City Trust, an urban renewal voluntary group associated with a local community and civil rights activist. Through their work a building was erected, which was later acquired by the City Council for the Tower Museum, which opened in 1992. The new museum was planned not only with both local people and tourists in mind, but also with the greater goal of making a contribution to 'cross-community mutual under-standing and reconciliation'.[34] Reflecting on that time, the Programme Organiser stated that the development of the museum raised a number of questions about developing a museum service in a divided city. It was necessary for them to consider, for instance, how a museum in a city like Derry might appeal to those who feel alienated by the political situation; whether tourism could be combined with the history of a city like Derry and still provide a creditable representation; and if the museum could address the difficulties of displaying such turbulent and controversial issues.[35]

Still, fifteen years later, the Tower Museum is the only museum in Northern Ireland to give space to the Troubles in its permanent exhibition, The Story of Derry. This exhibition began by considering archaeological evidence in the area and then went on to provide the history of the city from its the sixteenth-century origins to the twentieth century. The part of the gallery to get the greatest attention was that on the history of the city since 1965, which included such controversial episodes as the Civil Rights movement, Bloody Sunday and the Hunger Strikes. The story of the Troubles was mostly told in a film on the history of the city, and cases were used to display objects associated with the conflict, such as a prisoner's letter and a plastic bullet.[36] This was a challenging display for Northern Ireland, both from a tourism aspect and from the perspective of attempting to interpret the conflict. An early version of the video on the history of the city was criticised as 'depressing' by the Northern Ireland Tourist Board, which provided part of the funding for the project, and was labelled as 'anti-Protestant' by others. Later, uproar surrounded the display of a real AK-47 Kalashnikov rifle and objections were raised against the use of an image of a masked republican gunman on the front cover of a promotional leaflet. A local Northern Ireland newspaper, *The Newsletter*, voiced its objections in an article with the headline 'Museum displays IRA gun', and a member of the Conservative backbench was quoted in *The Times* as describing the museum as 'perpetuating the propaganda of the IRA'.[37] Despite these early problems, the museum did gain more general acceptance from the two communities. In the words of Desmond Bell, who has written on the development of the museum, an 'approving visit' from Ian Paisley, leader of the Democratic Unionist Party, at the opening ceremony, 'seemed to set the loyalist seal of approval for the venture'.[38] Praise also came from the museum community: in 1993 the Tower Museum was 'specially commended' by European Museum of the Year Awards and was named Irish Museum of the Year.[39]

Good relations at the Tower Museum, Derry/Londonderry

In 2007 the Tower Museum has now entered a new phase in its development. Aided by National Lottery funding, its permanent galleries have been expanded to include finds from the Spanish Armada, which was wrecked off the nearby Irish coast. In addition, the galleries on the history of the city have been refurbished and redisplayed. The closure of the museum for a period to develop these new exhibitions allowed staff the opportunity to explore new areas. On this occasion this was the development of the Good Relations Programme, funded by the District Council's Community Relations Programme. The Programme is an educational resource that uses local history to explore citizenship and community relations themes and is made available to schools, and to youth and community groups. The initiative has three elements, each of which can be used as the basis of separate visits: printed trails linked to exhibitions that explore the ideas of local and global citizenship; a CD-Rom that provides an interactive journey through the history of the city; and a hands-on interactive activity using boxes containing real and replica objects. The objects have been selected to trigger discussion on how history can impact on our attitudes and viewpoints.

However obvious it might seem to people in museums and cultural centres elsewhere, such a direct museum programme relating to community relations is an innovative, and even precarious, departure for a museum in Northern Ireland. The project is innovative because no museum has until now developed a permanent programme on such a scale that tackles issues relating to the conflict. It could be considered precarious because of the high levels of skills and training required to deal with a subject of such sensitivity in a city that has seen some of the worst events of the Troubles. Discussion of such matters has often been avoided in museums, schools and other areas of public life for fear of an inability to address the issues that would be raised. This was kept in mind during the development of the Good Relations Programme. The various aspects of the Programme were subject to two years of planning, staff training and evaluation. Community relations training was provided for all staff, including gallery attendants. Prior to training, a baseline survey was undertaken to find out staff attitudes to community relations work and their levels of past training in areas such as equality, cultural and religious diversity, conflict resolution, group facilitation, citizenship and mediation skills. Information was also gathered on how equipped staff felt to listen to experiences of the Troubles, fear and discrimination. They also asked how confident the museum staff felt about discussing such experiences and dealing with controversial issues of that nature. Responses were used to facilitate workshops for museum staff addressing these areas. As a result of workshops, staff felt they had gained new skills. One responded by saying: 'I learnt to listen, to see and to think.' Another said she had learnt 'to think about different points of view and how we all see things differently'. There was also evidence of support for further work: one member commented, 'there is a lot more the museum service can and should be doing for community relations'.[40] As a result of these initial training days a number of staff have gone on to further training in this area and two have gained an Advanced Open College Network (OCN) certificate in conflict resolution skills.

The Tower Museum Good Relations Programme has been deliberately designed to tackle issues of identity, conflict, community and the idea of a shared future in Northern Ireland. As the result of collaboration between the Education Officer at the Tower Museum and the Community Relations Officer in Derry City Council, the programme has been created in the context of, and as a contribution to, the policy document *A Shared Future: Policy Strategic Framework for Good Relations in Northern Ireland*. Published by the Office of the First Minister and Deputy First Minister in March 2005, this report has moved away from the idea of 'community relations' and towards the promotion of 'good relations' as a means to the establishment over time of what the report refers to as 'a normal civic society' in Northern Ireland. This civic society is to be one in which individuals are 'equals' and differences are resolved through dialogue, and is aiming for the formation of a society where there is 'equity, respect for diversity and a recognition of our interdependence'.[41] Thirteen policy objectives are named as means to achieve these ends. These include: the elimination of sectarianism and racism; the promotion of civic-mindedness; the development of a shared community and encouraging understanding of the complexity of our history through museums and schools.[42]

Good relations and the museum sector

The Department of Culture, Arts and Leisure (DCAL) in Northern Ireland has asked museums, libraries and archives to explore history, to support cultural projects that look at the complexity of identity, and to 'develop cultural capital' through learning. *A Shared Future* clearly sets out an agenda for Northern Ireland's museums (see Table 6.3),[43] which includes ensuring collections represent diversity, that exhibitions represent the community the museum serves, and that education or outreach work responds to cultural diversity.

More recently 'an action plan' has been published to provide guidance on how to implement the above objectives.[44] Again, recommendations are made, such as using the cultural sector to 'highlight the multifaceted and overlapping nature of identities and their wider global connections and encourage understanding of the diversity of our shared history'. However, this document, like the one published a year earlier, provides no guidance on how this should be implemented, how

Table 6.3 How museums (in Northern Ireland) should contribute to good relations policy

Ensuring that the collections are representative of the diversity which both has been and is present in the geographical area from which local visitors come and those places and domains which represent their interests, affiliations and concerns

Ensuring that both permanent and temporary exhibitions represent and examine the interests of all the communities that the museum chiefly serves

Devising exhibitions and supporting educational programmes/outreach work which address issues pertinent to the cultural diversity of the geographical area served

terms should be interpreted or what additional resources could be made available to meet the above agenda. The responsibility for furthering the agenda is held by the Department of Culture, Arts and Leisure (DCAL). In relation to the work of museums, DCAL turns to its colleagues in the Northern Ireland Museums Council (NIMC), which supports local museums, and the national Museums and Galleries, Northern Ireland (MAGNI) to communicate the latest policy recommendations. NIMC has responded positively and has for a number of years valued the importance of supporting and developing a community relations and later a cultural diversity awareness amongst its members. Most recently it has sponsored a cultural diversity exhibition that toured museums in 2005–6. NIMC is acutely aware, however, of the difficulty many museum staff have in the field of keeping up-to-date with current policy recommendations and statutory requirements, building these into their programmes and work, and finding the resources to respond quickly to new demands. On occasion, the Council has found, the constantly shifting sand of Government policy leads to confusion, weariness and cynicism within the museum sector, which those close to Government departments have to respond to.[45]

Are the initiatives useful?

The actual impact of museum activity on community relations is almost impossible to quantify; as noted by one commentator, 'if reports, conferences, exhibitions, think-tanks and books were enough, the Northern Ireland question would have been solved long ago'.[46] Measuring impact, both in the community relations sector and in the museum, is a growing concern and one that has had greater attention despite the difficulties posed by the practice. The Northern Ireland example helps to complicate investigations into the impact museum initiatives may have on improving community relations, understanding diversity and celebrating difference. It causes us to ask whether museums are being visited by those most closely involved in sustaining division; if they do visit, what do they gain from their experience; and can a museum visit have a long-term impact on deeply held views? Research has shown that it is often the visitor who has the most influence over what is learnt from an exhibition, rather than the curator or designer. Visitors bring their own personal experiences, histories and beliefs to the exhibition and it is through these that they will interpret the exhibitions. In addition, commentators working on evaluation and the impact of community relations programmes in Northern Ireland suggest that research tools are not yet sensitive enough to detect change; that changes only become apparent over a longer period of time; and that positive changes can only occur if a number of other conditions are met.[47]

However, some indication of the success of museum initiatives in Northern Ireland must be found in the fact that they continue to receive support from various community relations bodies. When considered together, the museum exhibitions, learning programmes and outreach do have resonance. Histories that were previously taboo and symbols that were misunderstood are now beginning to be discussed in public and secure spaces. These initiatives are thought to provide important learning events, which will stand out in people's memories. Reviewing education and community relations in Northern Ireland, Smith and Robinson refer to the value of positive 'formative events in peoples biographies'. With regard to early years education, they state that positive experience between different groups can have a significant long-term impact.[48] The potential positive impact of such visits is also supported by the work of Keith Barton and Alan McCully. They have considered the contribution of history teaching in shaping identity and are confident that well-managed community relations programmes in schools and with museums can and do impact on people's perceptions of themselves and others.[49] They challenge the usual assumption that what students learn in formal settings, such as schools and museum visits, is then over-shadowed and dominated by what they learn in social or community situations. Rather, they believe students construct their historical understanding through a range of interactions, including what they learn in school. In their study of history teaching in Northern Ireland they found that younger children's understanding of the past was not so politicised as often assumed and that older students did not often have the rigid stereotypical views of history that many expect. They also found that students, as they progressed through secondary school, often began to intensify their connections with unionist or nationalist narratives. Because students enter with a more flexible understanding of history, and in later years are constantly forming and re-forming their identities, Barton and McCully believe that such initiatives have the potential to play a critical role in helping students to widen their identifications and to develop new ones 'grounded in tolerance and mutual respect'.[50] It is on such a basis that museum staff in Northern Ireland who are responsible for community relations projects continue with their work. However, as they do so, there is a need for greater evaluation and scrutiny, as has been the case in relation to museum practice and social policy elsewhere.

7

Museums and community movements

Museums have long been associated with the social or political agendas of one group or another. Analysis of their history has uncovered the ideological foundations of our national museums, for instance, and the desire for power and privilege to be generated and replicated through museum displays. The examples of community groups, discussed in this chapter, who have been motivated to create their own museums reveal that exhibitions are being mounted, collections created and museums developed as a means to communicate an ideological message. These community groups are engaged in various forms of social activism and in these cases this relates to aspects of improving social and economic conditions, the promotion of a more democratic society, fostering understanding between groups, and community regeneration. The missions of these groups often relate to the concept of empowerment and the various principles implied by this approach, such as fostering conscientisation, advocating self-help and creating opportunities for user-participation. The examples discussed in this chapter show that community groups are using museums and heritage as a means to achieve these aims. The groups have recognised the potential of museums and heritage to have an impact on social and political conditions and are prepared to use it.

What is essentially different about the discussion within this chapter, which separates it from the approach that views museums as a means to enable state-approved community development discussed in previous chapters, is that it is based on initiatives that originated from within the community, rather than having been brought to them. In many cases, the examples discussed below are of socially and politically active groups who are engaged in a number of transformative activities, and the museum and heritage projects simply represent one of many tools created as a means to this end. To understand why these community groups have chosen to use museums and heritage as one of their aids is essential to this chapter. To grasp that means that we will have a better appreciation of what this example of community-based users perceive as being the potential of museums and heritage. It will explain the relevance of heritage at a community level, according to the groups that initiate the link. This chapter focuses on a particular aspect of the relationship between museums, community and heritage and reveals that heritage can become a social and political aid for groups whose goals and methodologies are distant from, and independent of, the official museum sector.

Heritage and the social movement

Continually, museums and heritage are being integrated with the community project as a form of social transformation. The issues of social capital, cohesion and inclusion discussed in previous chapters are examples of this. This chapter takes a different approach: it is still one that can be labelled as 'social transformation', but it is a desire for change coming from within a different process. The community groups that provide the material for this chapter are all engaged in various forms of social activism and have chosen to include heritage activity as one means to achieve this end. In each of the examples discussed, a heritage project, which has included museum-like activities (the creation of collections and display), actively contributes to these goals. The groups discussed each exhibit forms of social activism that reflect the ideals of New Social Movements (see Chapter 2). Central to the work of the community groups are issues of rights, justice, democracy and equality. The examples are also linked by the fact that each includes a heritage dimension to their work. The first example is a community education project, whose aim was to foster 'a radical social movement' that combined local community action with larger social concerns.[1] The second example is part of a movement whose goals relate to social justice, cultural identity and land rights. The third is a community council whose mission is to achieve 'human rights, social justice and economic equality'.[2] Each is concerned with the notions of empowerment and community conscientisation.

In addition to having distinct characteristics, the social movements of the twentieth century have also gone through their own life stages. Herbert Blumer, writing in the 1950s, explored the nature of these life stages, and his work still has relevance today. He suggests that the movements go through four stages. The social movements begin with a period of social unrest or agitation. Leading from this is a period of popular excitement, which develops a sense of belonging and raises morale. Later this interest is formalised through the development of an ideology associated with the social movement. Finally, through the formation of operating tactics, the movement is institutionalised.[3] These points are important because they recognise that social movements are not static interests; rather they evolve through time. At each point the movement will have different needs according to whether it is an emerging movement or one that is more established. What will become clear below is that the relevance that heritage or museum activity will have for the social movement will depend on the stage the movement is in. The characteristics of the different stages, and how they use museums, will also reveal something of how the museum functions. At each time the museum will take on a different role and will be used to express differing needs and aspirations – each revealing the malleable nature of how museums and heritage are employed.

Community education: Ulster People's College, Belfast

For the community groups discussed in this chapter heritage activity is used as a means to achieve social change. The exhibitions or museums generated by this activity were products of processes that had other goals in mind. The groups may well have embraced numerous methods to communicate their message; nevertheless, in every case the goals of social, economic or cultural development remained the same. This first example is that of the Ulster People's College in Belfast, a grass-roots community development organisation established to bring about social and economic change through education. The college has developed numerous teaching programmes, in areas such as community relations and community development. The one of most interest to this study is a heritage project centred on a programme titled 'People's History'.

An important theme in contemporary approaches to community education and learning is the relevance it has for concerns such as social participation and inclusion, as well as social justice, democracy and citizenship. Globally, community learning is high on the agenda for social and economic reform. Promoted through community schools, adult education colleges and national and local government strategies for lifelong learning, 'community learning' is now fully integrated into state policy. However, community learning is traditionally associated with more radical social agendas found on the outside of mainstream education provision. The example of a community education initiative discussed in this section originates from the work of community activists, trade unionists, community educators, peace workers and feminists who were 'openly committed to radical social change'.[4] The example is associated with a social movement that aimed to combat local experiences of sectarianism and to search for peace and justice. It is certainly an example that reflects the view that education is not a neutral process. Instead, education has the potential to be an instrument that either can be used to justify and normalise the social and political systems, or can be a means to bring about social transformation.[5]

The work of the Ulster People's College, which was established in 1982 in Belfast as a joint enterprise between trade unions, academics and community organisations, has been represented as embracing the Freirean notion of 'Cultural Action for Freedom'. This particular aspect of Freire's thinking was considered particularly useful because, in the words of one of the college founders, it encourages 'examination and exploration of people's communities in all their complexity' so as to enable people's sense of 'identity, integrity, security and dignity' to improve.[6] The Freirean approach to learning is reflected in the College Mission Statement, which embraces the transformative potential of education and how it can be used to change social conditions:

> The Ulster People's College seeks to contribute through education, training and development to a just, democratic and non-sectarian society with improved social and economic conditions and participation for those who have been disadvantaged and excluded.[7]

111

The College's description of its work reflects many of the ideals of the work of Freire and Gramsci, as discussed in Chapter 2. Through a range of community development programmes the College aims to make a positive contribution to the difficulties that have arisen from cultural, educational and political exclusion. In its response to the Government document *A Shared Future Policy and Strategy Framework for Good Relations in Northern Ireland*, published March 2005,[8] the College stated its position with regard to this new approach. The College sees itself as a place that can, through education programmes, foster good relations, promote equality and human rights, and enhance community development. The latter the College defines as 'intrinsically linked to the principles of empowerment, understanding and respect for diversity, equality, human rights and empathy'. In its response the College seeks for Government to investigate the very nature of the system in Northern Ireland that lays the foundations of suspicion, prejudice and alienation.[9] The College is making an active commitment to fostering social change in Northern Ireland. It is clear that the education projects developed by the college are still, over twenty years since its foundation, directly linked to the original Gramscian notion of cultural action for freedom.

In a city where the expression of identity and interpretations of history are so contested, the College refers to the value of providing 'opportunities for progression' and 'a safe and secure environment' in which the students can develop. The programmes offered by the College relate to the nature of experiences in Northern Ireland. For instance, through a number of different programmes the college aims to explore, with the students, 'the structural forces responsible for inequality, discrimination and prejudice', which for some have significantly shaped their lives. The philosophy and approach of the College also reflects key ideas in community development. The College prospectus for 2002 describes teaching methods that aim at 'encouraging greater participation by local people in decisions that affect their everyday lives', 'promoting networking and partnership' and 'broadening horizons, developing understanding and increasing solidarity'. The aim is to 'strengthen the capacity of groups'.[10] Tom Lovett, one of the people key to the foundation of the College, interprets this as 'an examination and exploration of people's communities in all their complexity in order to encourage the embracing of options, which improve people's sense of identity, integrity, security and dignity'.[11] The concerns highlighted by Lovett, and found in the prospectus, are recurring priorities, found in a range of contemporaneous Government policy and documents. However, the context of these claims coming from the Ulster People's College is very different, with the possibility of a different objective in mind.

People's History Initiative

These various accounts of the purposes of the Ulster People's College each provide a flavour of its goals for community change and how it still reflects the social movement from which it originates. Education is used as a means for people to develop critical skills to assess and challenge their social conditions. The diverse range of programmes reflects what the college has identified as the areas in greatest need. In 2000 these included community development, community economic development, community leadership, equality, rights and justice, and culture and identity. The short description of the latter states its aim as to 'assist imaginative exploration of identity and new ways of creating solidarity and winning change'.[12] This approach forms the People's History Initiative, which has been part of the college's work since the early 1980s. This course is described as an exploration of the history of local communities 'by examining the broader social, economic and political context in which communities develop and change'.[13]

Both Gramsci and Freire emphasised the importance of the study of community history because for a community 'to assume its role in the perennial struggle for liberation from oppression, it must know by whom it was preceded'.[14] The college invites community groups to engage in a range of history-based programmes that encourage people to investigate how their community constructs its own history, and what people choose to remember and share, or prefer to forget. Participants are given the opportunity to tell the story of their community in photographs, as well as in written and spoken memories. People are also encouraged to reflect on their findings about the past and use this in future plans for their community. The Initiative encourages participants to take control of the representation and interpretation of their community and allows them to explore historical themes relevant to their community. Together the group forms either an exhibition or a CD-ROM based on the community's history. The exhibition is placed on public display and the CD-ROM remains as a resource held within the group.[15] The aims of the Initiative (Table 7.1)[16] demonstrate the context within which the history project has been developed; the concern is to use community history to enhance personal skills, plan for the future and improve relations. The emphasis within the People's History Initiative is the provision of opportunities for groups who normally feel powerless and weak to represent their own experiences in a public setting. This is woven through the workshops and resulting exhibitions of each participant group.

Table 7.1 People's History Initiative: project aims

To use the community history of the recent past as a tool to encourage critical self-reflection, debate and dialogue within and between communities

To enhance conceptual and practical skills, at different levels, in a structured manner in both a single-identity and cross-community context

To enable communities to use their examination of the past to accommodate the present and plan for the future

To encourage socially excluded groups to explore and present their past

To utilise the People's History approach to support and encourage relationship building between groups and communities

To develop a sustainable approach to promoting a community relations/community education/community development model of community history

To develop further innovations in using a People's History approach to community relations and community development

The People's History Initiative is an example of how a heritage-based initiative has been used to achieve social change within communities. The Initiative has been funded by the European Structural Funds 2000–2006 EU Programme for Peace and Reconciliation Measure 2.1, which is concerned with 'Reconciliation for Sustainable Peace'. The purpose of this programme is to address the legacy of the conflict and to take opportunities arising from peace. The programme supports projects that demonstrate how they will 'develop reconciliation, mutual understanding and respect between and within communities'. The communities targeted must be those that show the effects of the conflict, have suffered community polarisation, and have been adversely affected by conflict and division. In its successful application for EU support made in 2000 the College outlined how the People's History Initiative fits such criteria. The Initiative is described as supporting and facilitating a process that contributes to peace building by addressing the legacies of the conflict, such as:

> Disempowerment; division between and within communities; educational disadvantage and the consequent need to build up knowledge and skills in communities; lack of opportunities to explore history, identity and culture in a more critical manner; and the need for a more developed community relations and community development infrastructure.[17]

The Initiative aims to address the above targets by engaging with socially excluded groups, developing their self-confidence and skills, and strengthening their participation in their communities and wider society. The approach is to examine with community groups how they view the past as a 'necessary prerequisite for imagining and planning for the future'. Single-identity work on issues of 'culture, history, identity and diversity' explored through community history courses and cross-community contact aims to promote reconciliation. The ethos, structure and activities of the Initiative are described as supporting 'mutual understanding, respect and reconciliation' and starting from a place that 'recognises both the reality and the importance of religious differences between and within communities'. From an educational perspective, the college promotes the advantages gained from increased confidence and skills, such as logical argument and critical reflection, as well as gaining a formal qualification.[18]

In Northern Ireland the EU Peace and Reconciliation funding is administered by the Community Relations Council (CRC), and in bi-annual reports to CRC the college provides details of the aims and objectives of the Initiative and achievements in relation to these. The reports provide a sense of the community the Initiative is targeting, the interpretation of community development that is employed, and the type of community skills that are enhanced. The communities involved in the People's History Initiative are 'people in disadvantaged groups and communities' who are at risk of social exclusion through educational disadvantage, living on a low income and unemployment, as well as other factors.[19] Groups that engaged in the Initiative have included senior citizens, women's groups, men's groups, a group for those with learning disabilities, and groups from areas that have suffered as a result of the Troubles. Almost half of the participants had no educational qualifications and those who did tended to be only at an initial level.[20] Each year the Initiative has set targets for groups such as the long-term unemployed, women returning to work, those above retirement age, people from interface areas and participants from rural areas, which they have generally met or exceeded.[21]

The key community development objective of the People's History Initiative relates to supporting and encouraging relationship building between groups and communities, using community history to promote community relations, community education and community development. The Initiative promotes single-identity work (which involves people exploring the history and culture of one community in particular, usually the one to which they belong), which will in some cases lead to collaborative cross-community work. Project materials and delivery aim to enhance community relations, and project evaluations have shown that people feel that their historical knowledge has been extended, beliefs challenged, and understanding of their own and other communities enhanced. Targeting groups that have experienced violence and polarisation has, according to project evaluations, succeeded in helping people to understand their own history and that of others, increased skills in discussing issues around the history and development of the conflict, and provided the tools to enter dialogue with other groups. Some of the most successful participant groups have requested a continuation of cross-community meetings long after the People's History workshops have been completed.[22] The college has also found that groups who initially were involved in single-identity workshops had, through increased confidence and skills, then participated in related cross-community collaborations.[23]

The People's History Initiative aims to develop community skills by encouraging people to explore the past in a way that encourages critical self-reflection, debate and dialogue. In many cases, participation has led to links being formed between the groups and local libraries and schools, and participants have often reported a greater willingness to progress to further learning (both within the college and outside it) and community involvement. One group is now developing a Community Archive and another has got involved in reminiscence work in a local primary school. Exhibitions developed as a result of the Initiative have often been displayed well beyond the end of the project, in community venues. From these various initiatives the programme has evidence that it has led to greater levels of community confidence. Groups have reported that they now feel more equipped to debate the history of their community and are more likely to engage in further educational and community activity. Participation in community exhibitions and the production of CD-ROMs has led to a greater sense of pride and energy. The launch of these products is described in project reports as 'positive occasions', which have promoted more constructive and affirmative attitudes.[24]

Community Exhibition, Newry, Northern Ireland

One such exhibition is that developed by a community association based in Newry, a city located close to the border between Northern Ireland and the

Republic of Ireland. This particular community development association formed in an area of the city that experiences very high levels of deprivation, as defined by the Northern Ireland Multiple Deprivation Measure 2001.[25] The measure is calculated on the basis of a number of variables, these being: income; child poverty; employment; health deprivation and disability; education, skills and training; geographical access to services; housing; and, lastly, social environment. This area of Newry was calculated as being among the 16 per cent most deprived areas of Northern Ireland. In order to tackle some of these measures of deprivation a Community Association was formed in 2002 with the aim to provide new opportunities for young people and increase a sense of community spirit and participation in the area. Through a range of activities the Community Association aims to bring new benefits to the area, to create positive relationships with local and national agencies, and to encourage the development of improved social, educational and cultural services. The activities undertaken by the Association included the establishment of a Heritage Committee.

In 2003 the committee researched and mounted a low-budget exhibition on the area of the city represented by the group (Figs. 7.1 and 7.2). Text was used to tell the eighteenth- and nineteenth-century history of the area, and the more recent past was told through a display of approximately 300 photographs, mostly taken in the 1950s and 1960s. The photographs depicted people outside their homes: children playing in the streets, teenagers occupied with their music or sport, and multi-generational family groups gathered together. Text on the use and reuse of buildings in the area focused on their early use as a barracks, the life of soldiers in the town, and the experiences of wives and families associated with the barracks. The social housing of the early twentieth century was described as 'run down tenements', which were dilapidated and 'virtually slums'. The impact of the Northern Ireland Troubles, post-1960s, was described as having taken 'the heart from the estate', resulting in high unemployment, low educational achievement and a generally negative image of the area. The recent work of the local Community Association was described as having 'brought hope to the area'.[26]

The exhibition was a means for the Community Association to articulate its goals of community development and social improvement. Through it the Association told of the 'hopes and aspirations for the future' and emphasised the importance of bringing people of the community together in order to reach common goals. Emphasis was placed on the value of improving access, relationships and opportunities. The exhibition was an opportunity to illustrate support the Association had received from numerous agencies in Northern Ireland, such as the Community Relations Council, the European Union Peace and Reconciliation Fund, and Newry and Mourne District Council, which is an indication of confidence and provides the group with some authority. The exhibition was also a means to bring the people of the community together; it was an occasion when members of the community could build relationships, reflect on life experiences, and make connections with agencies prepared to support their work.

Figure 7.1 Photographs on display in the community exhibition, Newry

In relation to making and defining history, the exhibition was an exercise in community autobiography and in this case the act of autobiography took on a number of roles. The exhibition was an opportunity for a local group to construct their own history, and to tell their story in their own way. Unearthed fragments of the history of their area, photographs belonging to different people and individual stories were used to tell a community's history. The exhibition was a means to construct a common history and evoke shared memories. This was obviously a local and personal history and one which would have been familiar to many who viewed it. In the display, rarely were the details of particular experiences told – the majority of the photographs were exhibited without any captions. It was obvious from how people viewed the exhibition and interacted with each other that the displays allowed for intergenerational reminiscence: mothers told sons about past friends, local dances and the games they played. The images provided an impression of past life and acted as a trigger

117

Figure·7.2 Artefacts on display in the community exhibition, Newry

for the making of memories. In places, the exhibition was also an act of commemoration: because of the Troubles many of the young men in the photographs are now deceased. The success of the opening night of the exhibition, which was attended by over 200 people from the Linenhall Area, was an indication of how welcome this initiative was. The display of photographs of everyday scenes added value to the ordinary. The commonplace became something that should be treasured, and the exhibition became a celebration of past achievements and a distraction from current concerns.

The Newry exhibition and others sponsored by the People's History Initiative are important acts of community curation. In every case the community groups select their own stories, choose the objects and images to place on display, and provide their own interpretation. The community makes its own decisions regarding preservation, selection, interpretation and display. This notion of community curation is an important one and is central to the philosophy of the Ulster People's College.

Community conscientisation: District Six Museum, Cape Town

Heritage activity can be an opportunity for a community to take control of the presentation of its own history and this brings with it numerous consequences. Those involved have recognised the sense of pride associated with displaying one's own story in a public space, and the value of nourishing group identities and establishing group bonds. One such example is that of the District Six Museum, a heritage project that has allowed a dislocated community to find a renewed sense of identity through place and shared experiences. Through this project the histories and experiences of a community have been made public and, rather than remaining unspoken, have become a building block to plan for the future. The global profile that the museum has now achieved is a demonstration of how community experiences can lead to national or international awareness and conscientisation.

The development of the District Six Museum in Cape Town, South Africa, is an example of community capacity building in a place torn apart by the separatist politics of apartheid. District Six is an area of Cape Town that was defined as white-only under the Group Areas Act of 1966. As a result of this Act, 60,000 people were forcibly removed from the area and their homes were demolished. With this move, people were distanced from their friends, family, jobs, schools and churches, and the community they had developed was broken. For many this was deeply traumatic. In the 1980s the 'Hands-off District Six' campaign, which aimed to protect the land from unsympathetic redevelopment, raised the idea of the creation of a museum as part of this process. In 1989 the campaign formed the District Six Museum Foundation and in 1994 the District Six Museum emerged (Figs. 7.3 and 7.4). This function is reflected in the museum mission:

> The mission of the Museum to District Six is to ensure that the history and the memory of forced removals in South Africa endures. It aims to foster understanding between communities, isolated by segregation, by focussing on the multicultural nature of District Six. Central to its mission is the documentation and imaginative reconstruction of the history, labouring life and cultural heritage of the District Six community.[27]

This mission conveys the fact that the museum has many roles: it is a memory project; it has an educational purpose; and it has a contemporary agenda. Each of these roles informs how the museum works, the people it represents and to whom it communicates. Each also reveals a particular relationship with the idea of community and the active role it takes in the expression of community.

As a memory project the museum aims to 'recall community' with the hope that it becomes 'a place where the memory of what had happened could be kept alive, a place were the descendants of the removed community could be told the story

Figure 7.3 Embroidering the memory-cloth at the District Six Museum, Cape Town

Figure 7.4 Tour underway in the District Six Museum, Cape Town

of District Six'.[28] As an educator, the District Six Museum tells the stories of forced removals throughout South Africa and invites these communities to make their contribution. The museum is also very much considered as an engagement with contemporary issues; it is a mode of expression and has an active part in the reuse of District Six. The development of a museum was a means to recapture the community spirit of the area, as an opportunity to generate support for the campaign to return the families who had been removed to the area. Since its opening, former residents of District Six have regarded the museum as 'a place to memorialise the history of the struggle' against apartheid, 'a living museum', and a space 'where stories can be told, where the layers of memories can be uncovered in an ensemble of hope'.[29] The museum was to 'engineer a collective spirit and a camaraderie'[30] and it was to be 'a community museum, an open museum, the people's museum'.[31]

The exhibitions at the District Six Museum

In the 1980s the District Six Foundation began by aiding the development of a number of 'itinerant' exhibitions in buildings around the District, which helped to generate interest and funding for the idea of a museum.[32] The museum began without any material collection, aiming instead to collect what the first curators referred to as 'the intangible spirit of community'. The first permanent displays, mounted in Buitenkant Street Methodist Church, which was to become the permanent home of the museum, concentrated on a revival of memories of the streets of the District. The exhibition Streets: Retracing District Six, core to the work of the museum between 1994 and 1998, led to the creation of maps, and collecting street name plaques and photographs, which were later to become key artefacts in the museum and were the first tangible remains of the area to be placed on public display.[33] Objects were found by chance: the street name plaques had been secretly saved by one of the workers involved in the demolition of the District and were later donated by him to the museum. Other objects were formed within the exhibition. For instance, visitors were encouraged to add their names to the floor map of the District, indicating where they lived. In a serendipitous moment, at one of the earliest museum events ex-residents were invited to write messages on curtain cloth, and these memory-cloths have become a key part of the museum process and exhibitions. These core objects of the Streets exhibition have taken on their own talismanic charm, reflecting both the vulnerability of the District and the resilience of its people. The rescued street name plaques reflect the fragility of streets and buildings, which normally appear so permanent. The floor map and the cloth reflect people's spirit, creativity and collective strength.

The more recent Digging Deeper exhibition, which opened in the renovated church in 2000, was so called because of its 'self-conscious and self-reflective' nature and its desire to 'tell the story of District Six with greater complexity'. A key purpose of this exhibition was to 'disrupt and unsettle certain conventions about the District', such as ideas of it being a 'coloured place' or a slum, and even to investigate 'our shames' and 'the hurts we inflicted upon each other'.[34] The physical exhibition is composed of professionally printed panels standing around the edges of the museum space, leaving the floor space free for the street map. A tower of street plaques is exhibited against one wall and a name cloth is draped from the gallery above. The panels make extensive use of oral testimony – most panels are written in the first person and share experiences of living in and leaving the District. The panels also have room for visitors to add text to the display. The openness of the museum space allows for visitors to be aware of one another, rather than to be closed off or hidden in a maze of exhibition panels. The exhibition space also includes 'memory rooms' formed by two reconstructed interiors and an area in which people can visit a sound archive. One of these memory rooms is a reconstruction of the family room of Nomvuyo Ngcelwane and it shows how a single space was bedroom, living room and kitchen. The exhibition includes her bed, table and chairs, kitchen dresser and stove.

In the Cape Town museum landscape, which traditionally reflects the European approach to museum building and display, the District Six Museum stands out as being very different. Here the building and space are modest; there are no glass cases; the curator has not taken authority; and the exhibition text is not fixed – former residents may add to the panels while they visit the exhibition. The entire exhibition, and especially the reconstructed rooms, makes use of people's memories as a means to stimulate connections, remind people of shared experiences and build community capacity by empowering individuals through telling their story publicly. Giving value to memories, no matter how simple and everyday, helps forge capacity by building links between individuals and experiences. It is created through the sharing process; the exchange of memories enables the building of links. The then Director of the museum, Sandra Prosalendis, emphasised the importance of these reconstructions. In relation to how the museum understands and uses memory, she commented:

> The memories provided this way become the histories that the museum is based on. This is a continually contested history and not necessarily the official interpretation. The people's memories become the museum's truth. The museum will not dispute an individual's memory. The house reconstruction is based on someone's memory. The house was probably far dirtier than how it was described to us. The person's memory has been selective, this is the way the person remembers it and we are going to respect that memory.[35]

For Prosalendis it is important that visitors understand that the Digging Deeper exhibition has not sanitised District Six; instead, 'we have looked for the values that were important for the people: cherishing the home, an inner sense of dignity. District Six was shabby but the exhibition is not shabby. Allowing memory to stand, that is someone's truth'.[36] Prosalendis has found that the museum has provided people with a sense of pride and has contributed to changing District Six as a symbol. Often presented as a place of poverty and gangs, now people are being reminded of friendships, good experiences and the dignity of the area. Rather than sanitisation, the museum sees this as revealing values that have gone unaccounted.[37]

The museum as part of a social movement

The museum was very much the product of a social movement that focused on rights, liberation and democracy. As a 'community-based independent museum', its function has been defined as 'to mobilise the masses of ex-residents [of District Six] and their descendants into a movement of land restitution, community development and political consciousness'.[38] Described as a 'period of heady protest politics',[39] the campaign needed to recover a sense of belonging for the people who had been dislocated and the museum was a means to do this. In a discussion of the museum's beginnings, one of the Trustees refers to it as originating from a movement that 'mobilised and re-energised' people to recover the District.[40]

It is not simply the fact that a museum of District Six opened that is relevant; what is far more interesting is why a museum should have emerged. The museum has become a space where people who formerly lived in District Six can come together and share past experiences. It provides an opportunity for people to 'recall community'. This community capacity building is based upon shared history and a clear sense of place. The museum exhibition draws on nostalgia for past lives and harnesses this sentiment as a vehicle for political change. In this example, the community has used the museum idea but revisited it and presented it anew. The example of the District Six Museum conveys very well the values associated with museums and, in turn, their power. The public and shared recollection of events in a museum space empowers and changes how that past is understood. What caused a person to feel shame now evokes pride; closed memories have now become open and shared; and a fragile people are becoming a stronger community. The District Six Museum is also an example of a community taking control of the presentation of its own history and this brings with it numerous consequences. Those involved have recognised the sense of pride associated with displaying one's own story in a public space, the value of nourishing group identities and establishing group bonds. By doing so the museum, and the activities it encourages, is providing opportunities for community empowerment and change.

This history of the Hands Off District Six campaign, and the museum that was a product of it, is a demonstration of the life stages of a social movement. This was a movement concerned with political struggle for 'human rights, freedom of association, of education, [and] freedom to elect'.[41] Early stages of a social movement are characterised by social unrest and agitation and in District Six this was the case from the 1970s when people began campaigning for the memory of the area to be preserved. Through a meeting, which was described as having 'mobilised and re-energised a whole range of people',[42] local activists generated the idea of forming a museum. What were described by early activists as 'itinerant exhibitions',[43] which could 'engineer collective spirit and camaraderie',[44] represent the second phase, that of developing belonging and raising morale. The social movement enters its third phase with the development of an ideology. Through the display of artefacts, photographs and memorabilia of individuals and families in the early exhibitions, the ethos of the museum was formed and shared. Maybe now, with the opening of the new exhibition in 2000 in the restored building, the museum is entering the final established or institutionalised phase. With the publication of *Recalling Community in Cape Town*, a volume that brings together the ideas and thinking of some of the key people in the development of the museum, the museum's history is formalised.

Since the 1980s the museum has been an integral part of the objectives of the movement of which it is a part. Ciraj Rassool, Professor of History at the University of Western Cape and a Trustee of the District Six Museum, regards the museum as 'an organisational device' that 'asserts a particular politics of governance and institutional orientation'. He believes that by doing so it expresses 'a particular commitment to social mobilisation, and to constructing and defending independent spaces of articulation and contestation in the public domain'. This, according to him, arises from the museum as a hybrid space for activist intellectuals, museum professionals and performers of the 'authentic voice'.[45] What he is revealing here is the very active political role the museum has taken. It is about turning a community around to challenge traditional modes of governance and assume some of that role for themselves. Through this mobilisation people are invited to speak out about their own experiences and wants. The museum was indeed an organisational device and brought people of the District back together to recover their histories and experiences as a means of planning for the future. Rassool notes, for instance, that the creation of the museum was regarded as relating to the establishment of the Truth and Reconciliation Commission, as a means to unearth the past and record memories.[46] The idea of the District Six Museum being a community museum is also deliberate – Rassool describes it as 'conscious and strategic'. In this way the museum is able to draw on the ideas of authenticity and representativeness, as well as being a 'locus for social organization and mobilization'.[47]

The story of the museum just described represents only the time since it was first mooted in the 1980s, and the life stages of social movements would normally stretch over a far longer period; nevertheless, using such an analogy to reflect upon the museum indicates well the life stages an innovative project like this has gone through. It demonstrates how the role of a heritage project, within a movement, will alter as the movement matures and its needs are meet. By the latter stages, and through the formalisation of knowledge in a permanent museum, the status and importance of the movement is established, recognised and stabilised.

Community empowerment: Falls Community Council, Belfast

The final example used in this chapter to explore how heritage has been involved in social movements is that of a community council that has been engaged in various forms of social and political activism. Falls Community Council was established in Belfast in the 1970s to represent the needs and rights of people living in a mostly republican area of Belfast. It sees itself as playing a key role in 'developing community infrastructure and harnessing community activity' in an area it believes has suffered from 'social injustice, economic discrimination and civic marginalisation'.[48] This is reflected in the mission statement of the Council, which focuses on achieving 'Human Rights, Social Justice and Economic Equality' by the means of 'Active Engagement with the process of Conflict Resolution, Political Transition and Social Transformation'.[49]

The language of the Council reflects that used in the literature of empowerment. The concern here is classically that of the new social movements of the twentieth century: minority rights, liberation and 'democracy from below'.[50] The processes are those of community conscientisation and transformative action. The aims of the Council are named as: community empowerment; participative democracy; active citizenship; social transformation; conflict resolution; and political transition. In a highly divided city, these aims are presented as focused on providing the people of the area with opportunities to 'gain the confidence, skills, knowledge and vision to actively engage in processes which will reshape society and bring about democracy and inclusivity'.[51] The Council makes it clear that central to this rationale, and the various projects that it has engaged in, is the realisation of empowerment, as well as the tasks of 'transforming society' and 'building lasting peace'. This thinking is encapsulated in the logo of the Council, a flower in which each petal represents one of the aims of the Council and each links to 'peace building' at the centre of the flower. Heritage projects have been given a similar profile to other aspects of development planning within the Council, such as education, community drugs programmes and community development support. The heritage projects have taken two forms: the creation of a community archive, which is regarded as phase one, and the proposal to establish a local museum based on the experiences and history of the local people, which brings the project into phase two. The developments have also been subject to an external feasibility study, supported by the Council in 1997, which made recommendations on how they might make a positive contribution to local employment, tourism and conflict resolution.[52] How the heritage projects have been woven through the aims of the Council provides insights into the museum and archive as a social instrument.

Duchas Sound Archive, Falls Community Council

Oral history is often regarded as a radical redefinition of established forms of history. By these terms established history is rejected as based on a tradition of state-approved historical documentation undertaken by professional historians recoding events and people important for the national story. This history has been perceived as being one dominated by the history of men and government. The recent focus on oral history has taken a different approach. This new method is one that is thought to be free of traditional constraints. Rather than being based on documentary evidence, it is mainly oral recordings that recount people's memories. Family or community members replace the trained historian; and local experiences, rather than national issues, are the main subjects. In the UK the Oral History Society describes this new practice as a means to enable 'people who have been hidden from history to be heard, and for those interested in their past to record personal experiences and those of their families and communities'.[53]

The oral archive developed by Falls Community Council, which is known as the Duchas Sound Archive, embraces this notion of oral history as a means to access the people's story. The archive is described as a 'living history project' that is recording experience of life in nationalist west Belfast since 1969. It is a multimedia history archive that contains oral recordings, photographs, documents and artefacts collected from people in the local community and 'not currently in the public domain'.[54] Emerging since the success and momentum of the sound archive as the 'flagship' is a second proposal from the Community Council to create the 'West Belfast Living History Museum' and a 'Conflict Resolution and Peace-Building Learning Centre'. Planning for the project in 2001 proposed that the Centre should present the history of the Falls community since 1969 and should house the sound archive as well as the catalogued personal reminiscence photographic archive, multimedia productions, exhibitions, website and education programmes. The Council has described the proposed 'Museum and Learning Centre' as a 'fitting memorial to all in our community who have suffered or lost their lives as a consequence of the political conflict over the past 30 years'. It also referred to its potential as a 'historical educational and research tool', a contribution to conflict resolution, aid to the development of 'political tourism', and 'legacy for the future'.[55] Both projects the Council believes will make an important contribution to the peace process, as a means of 'recording and preserving for prosperity, the suffering and experiences of this community' in an area that has 'disproportionately endured the trauma of the violent political conflict'. This is advocated on the basis of the belief that 'remembering the suffering of the past' is part of the process of engaging with change.[56]

The very act of contributing to the archive, and engaging in the processes of collecting, listening and sharing, is presented as making a positive contribution to peace and reconciliation. By 2001 over eighty interviews had taken place since the archive was established in 1999 and approximately half of these were made available to be read or listened to. Visitor response to the sound archive has drawn on the value of sharing these memories and the importance of allowing those who have experienced the conflict to speak out. Originally interviews focused on key experiences of people in the area, such as the 1960s civil rights campaign, internment and the 1981 hunger strikes, as well as the experiences of women during the conflict.[57] More recently the archive has adopted a 'life history approach' that has attempted to take greater account of an entire range of personal experiences.[58] This has provided a better understanding of the contributors and their interpretative framework. It has also provided further perspectives on other forms of social, economic and cultural histories (see Table 7.2).[59]

The epistemology of oral history, the fact that this is a radical rethink of the sources and methodologies of history, suits the objectives of Falls Community Council. The purpose of the Council is to bring about change in Northern

Table 7.2 Summary of strategic objectives of the Duchas Sound Archive

Depict the political, social, economic and cultural history of the area

Enable the people of the area to contribute individually and collectively to the historical record

Support and develop a process of active engagement in recording history

Explain the political conflict in the area through presentation of archive materials

Establish an interactive Living History Museum and Conflict Resolution and Peace Building Centre for Learning in West Belfast

Ireland, change that will question established and state notions of the management and administration of Northern Ireland. A new definition of what is history, and whose stories should contribute to it, could help further this agenda. The ethos of the oral history sound archive, and the uses the Council wishes to make of it, is well conveyed in a Memorandum submitted in April 2005 by Falls Community Council to the Select Committee on Northern Ireland Affairs established to investigate ways of dealing with Northern Ireland's past that would contribute to intercommunity healing. In this document the purpose of the oral history work was presented as 'enabling our community to make sense of the past we have experienced'. The Council presents its belief that 'grassroots engagement with the process of recording history is a means for peacebuilding and political transformation'. Through their experience to date, the Council informed the Select Committee that there is 'no necessary or inevitable link between telling and healing'; instead, collecting oral history is a very individual process that must take special care of the contributor. Furthermore, oral history is described as providing benefits that, if treated responsibly, could become 'gifts to the transition to a just and peaceful society'.[60]

Oral history as a project of Falls Community Council very much reflects the needs of the organisation and the context in which it is operating. The conceptual foundations of oral history are very suited to the objectives of the Council and reflect its concerns. The importance of pursuing democracy and inclusivity, as noted in the Council's Development Plan, is reflected in the rationale and methodology of oral history work. Claire Hackett, coordinator of the archive, describes oral history as being concerned with 'giving a voice to those most marginalized'. She values it as a means to 'challenge concepts of power and authority' and to hearing the stories of people 'who are usually ignored in official accounts'.[61] Furthermore, Hackett considers that the need for the sound archive arises from the social and cultural conditions of Northern Ireland. The archive, she states:

> stemmed from a desire to recount a history that has not yet been told and in doing so contribute to a process of political and social transformation. As a history of conflict and war it seems to me that the issues of power and authority are thrown into strong relief with the risks of speaking out still very immediate for many of our potential contributors.[62]

Issues of power and authority in Northern Ireland have been contentious, with whole communities feeling that they have been deprived of political influence and acknowledgement. In this case empowerment of a group that feels marginalised is crucial to its future. Furthermore, the very idea of challenging authority is vital to the work of the Council which would be underpinned by a desire for a independence from British rule. In this example the creation of an oral history archive is integral to the community development work of a community-based organisation. This has impacted both on the nature of the archive and on how the development work was undertaken. The fact that the archive is part of a community development organisation is considered by Hackett to be 'one of its greatest strengths'.[63] In the Memo to the Northern Ireland Select Committee this partnership is described as 'an alternative community development approach'. The Council considered that this new approach improved on overarching state-led approaches to peace building, which did not take account of the diversity of contested narratives of the past. The archive and proposed museum are examples of heritage activity that has been integrated with this approach and has brought additional perspectives to our understanding of the purposes of community heritage.

The approach taken by Falls Community Council can be compared to another community heritage initiative in Northern Ireland – the creation of 'The Museum of Free Derry', which has the subtitle 'The National Civil Rights Archive'. The museum opened in Derry in 2006 and has its origins in an exhibition developed by the Bloody Sunday Trust. Established in 1997, the Bloody Sunday Trust describes itself as a community-based education and history organisation that aims to explore the troubled history of the city 'as a means of enhancing respect and understanding for Human Rights, and promoting mutual understanding through the honest examination of our past'.[64] For a number of years the Trust hosted an exhibition and from that time there was greater awareness of the potential of public display. As with the Duchas Archive, the purpose of the Museum of Free Derry is to invite people to uncover a history that a community has felt has been hidden. The museum claims to provide 'the community's story told from the community's perspective, not the distorted version parroted by the Government and the media over the years'. Based on a large archive of artefacts and oral histories, it aims to express local identity, be an educational tool, preserve the history of the area and contribute to the local economy. Its founders have declared 'the museum will not just be a collection of artefacts and documents, but will be an active part of the local community'.[65] This example reinforces the idea of community heritage as a forum for alternative histories, voices and experiences. In these examples the highly politicised nature of community comes into direct contact with the contested nature of heritage and heritage construction. This is a highly volatile situation in which the issues of how community is being interpreted, and whose heritage is being represented by whom and for what purpose, are paramount.

The value of museums to social movements

Engagement with heritage, such as the creation of exhibitions and collections, has often been thought of as empowering – the examples I have just shared with you each appear to bring benefits to the communities involved with them. They might be considered empowering because of their contribution to making people more confident in their identities; the enhancement of a sense of civic duty brought through public participation; and the creation of new circuits of power by allowing people to tell their own story in public spaces. First we need to ask what motivates people to place these collections on display and present them as the shared material culture of a group. As noted already, one of the most potent instigators for community is insecurity.[66] Community is constructed when a group of people perceive an external threat; they come together as a means of self-defence. In each of the cases given above, external threats were perceived and shaped approaches. Under such conditions community activity may enhance a perceived sense of threat when it may not exist to that extent. Secondly we need to be aware of the impact of community initiatives that will tighten bonds within one community at the expense of others. In the case of the Northern Ireland examples, the collections were open to the public, and the organisers emphasised that all are welcome. But neither is likely to be visited by people unless they consider themselves members of the communities the exhibitions represent. Non-members would not have the cultural knowledge to interpret the collections or the social experience to feel at ease in the spaces where the exhibitions were held. The exhibitions will bring community members closer together, and reinforce a sense of exclusion for non-members. As a result of this, the exhibitions can also be seen as symbolic activities that mark the boundaries between communities and strengthen the relationships of those on the inside.[67]

The discussion of the construction and use of museums and heritage provided in this chapter has significance for our understanding of the operation of social movements, the construction of community and the meanings of museums. Social movements can be characterised by the formation of allegiance, the creation of a leadership and the establishment of set values, each of which has relevance for the examples discussed above. For social movements to form and successfully strive they need to develop a profile and create a sense of belonging and pride. They also need to form an ideology that is shared and provided with a sense of permanence. The heritage projects in this chapter have been an approachable way to communicate the messages of the movements. A shared history helps to form a sense of belonging and commitment to the social and political agendas of the movements. For examples in this chapter, display changed the meaning of that history and contemporary attitudes to it. The telling of the story of District Six created pride, the Newry exhibition brought new hope, and the Duchas Archive is thought to be a legacy for the future. Taking control over the production and dissemination of knowledge about the past, and giving that knowledge a sense of permanence through the museum, brings strength to the objectives of the movement.

The community that is essential to the success of the social movements is formed through symbolic action. Understanding of the heritage or history of that community, and their experiences, serves both purposes. In these cases, the museum and heritage projects have served to make people aware of the history and traditions associated with their community. Whether the purpose is achieving social change, community conscientisation or empowerment, the telling of history, or more accurately the construction of a heritage, can play a part. This history takes on a symbolic role that will define members, create distinctiveness and form boundaries. Together the community is invited to rediscover their experiences as a means to bring them together to take an active role in their future. Through telling the history of the community, group leadership evolves and establishes itself. The heritage resources are, in these cases, resources used by communities for social action. Anthony Cohen, in his discussion of the symbolic construction of community, notes that 'for most people, at most moments of history, the past is inchoate, transmitted only selectively according to contemporary purposes'.[68] This has been the case of the examples discussed in this chapter: the communities and their agendas are both constructed through the public presentation in exhibition, museum or archive.

The idea of the museum and public display are relevant to the social movement. The association with the idea of a 'museum', and the assumptions this brings, as well as inclusion in public display all have their own power. In these cases, the very fact that we tend to ascribe the museum with authority and influence is useful for the social movement. Each of the examples of heritage activity presented in this chapter is outside the 'official' museum sector, and as independent initiatives each in its own way challenges the traditional idea of a museum, in the terms of how whose story is told, how items are collected and the method of display. By doing so the community groups are not only challenging the traditional hegemony of the museum, but are using it for their own purposes. The social movement is using the authority of the museum, and that provided through display, as an opportunity to further its needs. The museum, in this current guise, is still exerting its influence.

Conclusion

It is an interest in museums that has driven this study, and the idea of community has been used as a means to access some of the meanings of contemporary museums. By doing so the book has provided perspectives on their importance as understood by those who work in museums, the significance placed on them by government agencies, and the worth ascribed to museums by a sample of community-based users. It is clear that the multiple meanings of museums are exposed by the many ways community can be understood. As we change place, context and person a different meaning of community is constructed and used for distinct and separate purposes. Community may be a concern for group identity; it may be a desire to gather people together to challenge established structures; or it may be an interest in communicating state policy in relation to social change. As the community changes, so too do the value and purpose of museums; each community constructs those meanings according to its own needs. To be of value, museums need to find significance within these communities – without those connections the museum and its collections will be of little importance. It is people who bring the value and consequence to objects and collections; as a result, if a museum cannot forge associations with people it will have no meaning.

This book has demonstrated that museums and heritage have been a significant process to convey community interests and this has shaped museum practice, our perceptions of the role of museums and how we plan for them in the future. Community, however it is debated, defined and reviewed, is a vital part of our life and, for some, museums, because of their contribution to cultural life, provide the connections between community concerns. The report *Culture Shock*, published in 2005 by clmg, a UK-based think tank for the cultural sector, is just one of the latest documents to emphasise this point. This passionate report focuses on what clmg thinks are the key issues in contemporary society: defining our identity; the sense of cohesion, formed by how we relate to others; and citizenship, which is presented as how we relate to the state. The authors link these issues with community, culture and museums. They argue that the contemporary concern for defining and creating belonging, which is crucial to community, is a concern with culture. Clmg presents culture as a chief means to understand community and to enable communities to understand each other.

The representation and exploration of culture (and its importance for community) is, for clmg, the raison d'être for museums. For them this is the answer to their question 'why museums?'

This final chapter will look at some of the perspectives on 'why museums?' that have been raised as a result of the links that are made between museums and community. The book has explored community from a number of perspectives. It has been considered as a product of people themselves, who have used museums and heritage to symbolise belonging and as a means to communicate to other members and those on the outside. Community has also been looked at from the civic perspective: as a link to the state and state priorities. It has also been explored as a political tool, engaged in the politics of empowerment, conscientisation and popular education. Each of these approaches has used museums in particular ways, and these have been explored in preceding chapters. When these perspectives on community are turned around they expose particular thinking about the role of contemporary museums. The 'why museums?' question is informed by the relationship between museums and community and is now considered with regard to the museum sector, the state and the people.

Why museums? A museum sector perspective

Clmg has provided one perspective on the 'why museums?' question and this will have been informed by its own position, both as a research agency for the museum sector and, in its words, as a 'campaigner for the unique role of culture'.[1] It is speaking as the advocate of museums. In direct language it addresses colleagues in museums and asks them to 'celebrate, discuss and understand *all* culture' as a means to foster tolerance, respect and understanding. Replete with examples of museums doing such work, and hints and tips for how this could be achieved elsewhere, the report is a plea to museums to get more involved with communities, with issues both at the core of communities and at their boundaries. Museums, clmg argues, have the potential to be the 'network to initiate, facilitate, mediate and communicate people's stories in pursuit of cohesion, identity and citizenship'.[2] The authors admit they may be asking museums to aim too high, but respond that it is better to have high expectations than low.[3] For clmg the meaning and value of museums lies in a belief that they are 'for people', can use real artefacts to engage and motivate, and are one of the 'few remaining neutral public places'. Clmg promotes museums as places that 'have nothing to sell but understanding', and 'are about the meaning of life', 'about stirring up emotions as much as soothing them'. Museums 'can challenge us', and 'can change lives'.[4]

This approach reflects the politics of progressive communitarianism – a policy of empowerment has been adopted, one that uses the museum to address social needs, democracy and social justice.[5] The progressive communitarian approach to museums is one that has grown popular in the UK museum sector and that has informed writing that promotes museums as places that can foster inclusion, tackle inequality and address discrimination. It is also one that has informed museum practice, such as the Open Museum in Glasgow and exhibitions hosted by the Nottingham City Museums and Galleries tackling topics such as sexual health and sexuality.[6] This approach is one that suggests that museums are only functioning properly if they can contribute to these contemporary concerns. It is also one that is being forwarded by some of the most radical thinkers in the museum profession. For such people, the contemporary concern is the life-blood of the museum and gives the collections their meaning. One possible outcome of such an approach is a belief that if museums do not address current issues they will have no purpose. 'Why museums?', from this perspective, is because museums can have influence – influence that brings about social change.

For the museum sector, the impact of community is one of questioning the relevance of collections, the nature of museum practice and the response of others to the museum. Certainly, this was at the heart of the AAM initiative discussed in Chapter 4. That is not to say that these questions would not have been raised without the incentive provided by community; in fact they most certainly would have. Instead, more often the questions have only remained amongst the most progressive, with others preferring the safety of established practices. With community so central to how we talk about audiences, the 'why museums?' question is reinvigorated. The complexity of community, the multiple ways of understanding community, and the awareness we need in order to take account of the dangers that lie in generalising, simplifying or even glorifying community, should also be central issues when assessing museums and their impact and purpose. Because of this complexity community cannot be taken for granted, and neither can the practice and impact of museums. As the culture of community is revisited, critiqued and assessed so too should be the culture of museums. The issues are linked and inform one another.

Why museums? A community perspective

The examples discussed in this book show that the responses to 'why museums?' that come from communities vary significantly. Community groups will assign a range of roles to the museum, which vary depending on their needs. The distinctiveness of each community leads to the formation of museums that reflects this uniqueness. Furthermore, there is often diversity within communities, which will lead to different readings of a local museum. The District Six Museum, for instance, although frequently described as a community museum, has also been referred to as a 'hybrid space'. The museum is a fusion of interests, combining, as noted by Rassool, 'scholarship, research, collection and museum aesthetics with community forms of governance and accountability, and land claim politics of representation and restitution'.[7] This range demonstrates that a museum can have many functions, either simultaneously, or shifting with time, person and situation.

Not only is the museum a place of 'intersecting histories',[8] it is also one of intersecting meanings. The meanings are built upon the idea of the museum or objects as a 'contact zone'. The dialogue forged by contact with museums triggers their significance. Heritage, interpretation and display become opportunities that have 'an ongoing historical, political, moral *relationship* – a power-charged set of exchanges, of push and pull'.[9] When the range of identities and stakeholders come together in the display space, attempting to interpret and represent valued heritage, the museum or object as 'contact zone' is animated. The identities represented through the selection of heritage are given voice and have impact. The energy emitted by this push and pull is at the core of the significance of museums. This meaning varies according to the individual and, crucial for this study, within the community.

For the community group, museum rationale is a concern that begins very much with the members and is shaped by their needs in the present and their perspective on the future. The numerous examples of community interest in museums and heritage cited in this book show that the concern is often one of communication: communicating a group identity to other members and to those on the outside. The freedom to communicate is shown to be empowering: the Anacostia Museum was a success because for the first time the African-American community in that area felt that they could share their own perspectives and their history. This factor was also significant to the relevance of the Open Museum and the example of the museum network in Oaxaca in Mexico. This also underpins the motivations behind the District Six Museum and the other community heritage initiatives discussed in Chapter 7. The freedom to speak for oneself, in a place where one will be heard, is one of the core strands of achieving a sense of empowerment. For the community groups referred to in this book the provision of the space for a public voice was the rationale for the museum.

Often, for community-based museum initiatives, the survival of the museum, although favourable, is not paramount. In fact, the eventual demise of the community museum might well not lessen people's achievements or go against their needs. This may be the case when a museum is used to define or bolster the identity of a group. When that is achieved, the museum has served its purpose and its importance diminishes. This has been the case in some instances of nation building. The museum can be used to build the nation, and the museum can help it become established once the independent nation is formed. Later, when the confident nation has been fashioned, the museum will either go into decline or have to find a new purpose. When communities forge heritage projects they may be important to galvanise the group, but once the community gathers momentum the need for such initiatives will lessen.

There are many examples of short-lived community heritage initiatives, which those in the museum or heritage sector may decry, simply because longevity is one of the characteristics that the museum sector values. In Ireland significant investment in museums that commemorate particular events has often been criticised because later, when the urge to commemorate that event has gone, interest in the museum has declined.[10] In these cases conspicuous commemoration has surpassed sustainability rationale. Commemoration, rather than being about remembering the past, is about expressing an opinion in the present. For such community groups, museums and heritage functioned as a means to communicate their needs and their politics. In Northern Ireland the sustainability of the numerous proposed community-based museums on particular aspects of the Troubles has come into question. Currently there are at least four museum proposals that have had significant investment, even at the feasibility stage.[11] In addition, there are numerous other private collections that relate to the Troubles that are getting greater public recognition. What is the 'why?' behind these museums? They are serving a purpose, even in these early stages. The case to create these museums, coming from different groups, is raising the profile of each of the communities concerned. Even if the community does not succeed in creating a museum, the campaign to form the museum will still have been a valuable process, because of its contribution to identity recognition. If a community museum wishes to maintain its relevance, it needs regularly to refocus and recapture significance within its community. This has been identified by the Open Museum in Glasgow. Once recognised as a leader in how UK museums can engage with their communities, fifteen years later the Open Museum needs to re-evaluate its purpose to maintain relevance. Current staff have recognised that the Museum must enter a period of review and renewal that will take account of more recent shifts in community demographics and needs, as well as the reorganisation of other local services.[12]

Why museums? A state perspective

In January 2006 the UK Culture Secretary Tessa Jowell addressed the Royal Geographical Society on the theme of capturing the value of heritage. The concept at the core of her paper was that of public value. Jowell made links between heritage, public value and public benefit; advocated the importance of the historic environment as a means of developing a public identity; and discussed the idea of public value as a framework for understanding heritage. Greater awareness of the public, Jowell argued, should then be translated into decisions about priorities for public policy, public spending and management.[13] Although Jowell based her address on the idea of public value, she admitted it is a concept that has not yet been properly defined. Definition may elude because public value is dependent on the perspective and purpose of the person explaining the term. In relation to museums, there are numerous points of view regarding the relations between the public and how a museum should be valued. Museum staff may assign public value according to how people use and respond to the museum; or they may argue for the public value of collections of high historical, aesthetic or cultural value held in perpetuity for the locality or nation, but perhaps little used by the public. For the community, public value may rest upon whether a museum reflects their priorities. For the state, public value will often depend on whether a museum contributes to state values. Studies of museum history have often concluded that this is the case, and for contemporary UK Government Ministers this is no different. Tessa Jowell demonstrated this point in her address to the RGS. She encouraged the museum and heritage sectors to embrace consultation as a means to 'ensure that our priorities are shared by the public'. She favoured community consultation as an opportunity to find out more about how the public relates to heritage, but also presented it as a means to communicate the Government agenda.

The numerous examples of community development-related initiatives, discussed in Chapter 3, follow this same trend. State support for museums has been explored in the UK context with respect to the current concern for greater community cohesion, sustainability and regeneration. The fundamentals of these concerns, the concept of bonds, are also central to the idea of social capital, popularised by Robert Putnam, and were often referred to in the Museums and Community Initiative led by the American Association of Museums. These ideas are also found in the 'community building' initiative in New South Wales, Australia, and reoccur in policy in relation to multiculturalism and the promotion of good community relations. In these instances the purpose of museums is being rethought in the context of communicating the goals of government. This seems to be most prevalent in the UK context, where the priorities of the Department of Culture, Media and Sport closely reflect those of the Labour Government. It would be unrealistic to expect DCMS to be independent; indeed, the lack of distance has been the basis of the occasional call for it to be abolished.[14] On the basis of this political and cultural context, local and central government bodies responsible for supporting museums are more likely to respond to the 'why museums?' question by relating it to policy priorities. As a result, one could argue that to complement that, and flatter their financers, museums have no choice but to involve with current social policy. This then provides the rationale for collecting, staff appointments and new exhibitions. In practice, however, as the examples discussed above show, very often the concerns of government have not been at odds with the priorities some within the sector are setting. Those in museums are not isolated from the trends in political thinking, and on occasion their own political and social leanings will be evident in their museum practice.

For those involved with the work of the state, museums are a means to communicate their concerns. For government bodies the purpose of arts, museums and culture will always be assessed according to their own perspectives, priorities and interpretation of the context. The state does not desire museums that challenge its position of power or priorities; instead museums should complement their authority. The history of museums has shown that this has always been the case. That this approach is still apparent today will hardly come as a surprise.

Museums as intersecting spaces

The cultural, community group and civic sectors each bring a different perspective on the purpose of museums, and these values intersect in the museum space. The museum is not therefore a single space; instead it is one with many layers, each of which is revealed according to the interrogative tools used. When the layers move across each other, and cause friction, the consequences may be an opportunity for innovation or, equally, a cause for conflict. At times, interest in community and community change has led to positive changes in how we think about museums, their purposes and the impacts they may have. At other times, when the needs and agendas of the stakeholders from each context are misunderstood, misrepresented or not engaged with, the tensions arising from collaboration between the museum and community sectors can be damaging. What is clear, however, is that the relationship between museums and community is highly important. It has caused the layer of opinion and relationships with museums and heritage to move and given rise to new ideas about the purposes and politics of museums.

Consideration of community also demonstrates that the purpose of museums is in constant flux. This is an expression of the lifecycle of museums and of what they represent. The ebb and flow of life means that the value of heritage will continually be shifting and the fate of museums will move with that. With every shift, the museum continues to be 'a power-charged set of exchanges'.[15] This book has demonstrated that community can be considered either as a lived experience or as a civic tool. In both cases the concern is with definition, boundaries and belonging. Community, in either form, uses museums and heritage as a means of communication and governance. Museums are a means for groups to exchange perspectives and communicate these to others. These perspectives have controlling qualities – membership of a community will involve some adherence to the values on display within the museum. Ability and influence have been ascribed to the museum, and all of the stakeholders will draw on these characteristics to give authority to the message they wish to communicate. To understand the links between museums and community it is essential to interrogate these values and their influence.

Notes

1 The appeal of community, museums and heritage

1 Used by Corsane 2005, 339.
2 Museums Australia Incorporated, Cultural Diversity Policy May 2000, available at www.museumsaustralia.org.au.
3 American Association of Museums 2002b.
4 Point made by Mark O'Neill, Head of Arts and Museums, Glasgow City Council. Email correspondence 'Social Inclusion in Scotland', 29 August 2006.
5 Leicestershire County Council Community Services, 2004.
6 Ministry of Culture website Ontario, available at www.culture.gov.on.ca, accessed 21 November 2005; Carter 1992.
7 For more information go to the Nova Scotia Department of Tourism, Culture and Heritage, available at www.gov.ns.ca/dtc, accessed 23 May 2006.
8 Simpson 2006.
9 Davalos 1998, 522.
10 Mpumlwana *et al.* 2002.
11 Karp 1992, 12.
12 James 2001.
13 James 2001, 343.
14 James 2001, 354.
15 Smith 1991, 62–70.
16 Sklenar 1983.
17 For case studies see Díaz-Andreu and Champion 1996; Kaplan 1996.
18 Crooke 2000.
19 Kaplan 1994.
20 Lowe 2000.
21 www.fermanaghtrust.org/fermanaghtrustcasestudies.htm#church, accessed 18 May 2004.
22 Regeneration of South Armagh. For more information see www.rosa.ie.
23 Thank you to Jeanatte Warke, of the Shared City Project Londonderry, for telling me about the group and giving me their publications.
24 Women into Irish History 2002.
25 Healy 2003.
26 Healy 2003, 17.
27 Cited by Healy 2003, 20.
28 Davis 2005.
29 Jones 2005.
30 Jones 2005, 103.
31 Miller 1998.
32 Peers and Brown 2003.

33 Dean 1994, 20.
34 Neilson 2003.
35 Mason 2005, 207.
36 Hooper Greenhill 2000, 568; Carbonell 2004
37 Kelly 2005; Kelly and Gordon 2002.
38 ICOM 2006.
39 Museums Association 2000. The American Association of Museums Code of Ethics (2000) does not use the word community; instead it refers to the public and society.
40 Nightingale and Swallow 2003.
41 Nightingale and Swallow 2003, 69.
42 Research Centre for Museums and Galleries (RCMG) 2002, 4, 9.
43 Cited in RCMG 2002, 12.
44 Extract from www.glasgow.gov.uk/en/Visitors/MuseumsGalleries, accessed 29 September 2006.
45 RCMG 2002, 14.
46 RCMG 2002, 22.
47 Murakami 2005, 61.
48 Weil, 1998, 258.
49 Mason 2004.
50 Sandell 2002, 7.
51 GLLAM 2000, 27

2   Understanding community

1   Cohen 1985; Anderson 1991.
2   Cochrane 1986, 51.
3   Gilchrist and Taylor 1997.
4   Sandell 2002.
5   See Amit 2002.
6   Delanty 2003, 2.
7   'Women of the World' was established in County Fermanagh, Northern Ireland, in the mid-1990s. Through cultural events, working with the local museum and newspaper coverage they have become a significant part of Fermanagh's culture.
8   Amit 2002, 1.
9   Cohen 1985.
10 Evans 1997.
11 Dawson 2002, 30.
12 Howell 2002.
13 These are the themes explored in Gray 2002 and Revill 1993.
14 Van der Veen 2003, 581.
15 Butcher 1993, 3.
16 Bauman 2001.
17 Butcher 1993, 3.
18 Schofield 2002, 664.
19 Brent 1997.
20 For a fuller discussion of the history of community development see Campfens 1997.
21 Campfens 1997.
22 Rahman 1995.
23 See for instance the Community Development Xchange (CDX), a UK not-for-profit organisation, whose website lists the core values of contemporary community development. (Formerly Standing Conference for Community Development) www.cdx.org.uk, accessed 15 August 2005. The CDX was established in 1991 and its membership includes local authorities, policy makers, academics and 'grass-roots' workers.

24 CDX, www.cdx.org.uk, accessed 15 August 2005.

25 Fraser 2005.

26 www.communitybuilders.nsw.gov.au/building_stronger/, accessed 23 August 2005.

27 www.communitybuilders.nsw.gov.au/download/premspeech.pdf, accessed 23 August 2005.

28 www.communitybuilders.nsw.gov.au/building_stronger, accessed 23 August 2005.

29 migrationheritage.nsw.gov.au, accessed 23 August 2005.

30 http://migrationheritage.nsw.gov.au/toolkit/contents.html, accessed 23 August 2005.

31 Mayo 2000, 48–61.

32 Martin 2004, 29.

33 Blumer 1951, 60–81; Scott 1995.

34 Adams 2003, 8

35 Mayo 1999.

36 Gramsci 1971 quoted by Mayo 1999, 36.

37 Brow 1990.

38 Freire 1972, 36, 62–6.

39 Mayo 2000, 6–7.

40 Mayo 1995, 6.

41 Bennett 1995, 91.

42 Bennett 1995, 91.

43 www.nemlac.co.uk/strategy.htm, accessed 7 November 2005.

44 Strom 2001. For further information on the Center see www.culturalpolicy.org.

3   Community development and the UK museum sector

1 Linley 2004.

2 Museums, Libraries and Archives Council, *Bulletin Produced for the Sustainable Communities Summit 2005* (available at www.mla.gov.uk).

3 Linley 2004, 8.

4 Linley 2004, 10.

5 National Museum Directors' Conference (NMDC) was established in 1929 and provides a forum for its membership to share information and work collaboratively. Burdett 2004.

6 Burdett 2004, 43.

7 Burdett 2004, 11–12.

8 Burdett 2004, 20.

9 Burdett 2004, 43.

10 Burdett 2004, 2.

11 Lev-Wiesel 2003.

12 www.homeoffice.gov.uk/comrace/cohesion/, accessed 2 September 2005.

13 Denham 2001, para. 10. Available at www.communities.gov.uk.

14 Denham 2001, 28.

15 Available at www.culture.gov.uk/NR/rdonlyres/5CE87526-274F-4671-8FC5-0D62F9B1C186/0/CommunitiesBooklet.pdf.

16 Tessa Jowell in DCMS 2004b.

17 Local Government Association 2004, Foreword.

18 This phrase is taken from the title of the Inter Faith Network Charter, *Building Relations with People of Different Faiths and Beliefs* (2003) cited in Local Government Association 2003, 10.

19 Local Government Association 2004, 61.

20 Brief descriptions of all of these projects are found in Local Government Association 2003, 61–4.

21 Strickson 2004.

22 Aslam in Strickson 2004, 43.
23 Kim Strickson, personal communication via email; see also Strickson 2004, 1.
24 Strickson 2004, 1.
25 Strickson 2004.
26 House of Commons 2005.
27 Office of the Deputy Prime Minister 2005b, 4 (these specific points are outlined in the section 'Our vision – sustainable communities').
28 Office of the Deputy Prime Minister 2005b, 8.
29 Office of the Deputy Prime Minister 2005b, 21.
30 Blair in Home Office 2004, 5.
31 Blunkett in Home Office 2004, 8.
32 The work of the Civil Renewal Unit is outlined at the Home Office website www. homeoffice.gov, accessed 17 October 2005.
33 The work of DCMS is outlined at www.culture.gov.uk.
34 As listed on the DCMS website www.culture.gov.uk, accessed 28 June 2006.
35 DCMS 2004a.
36 DCMS 2004a, 4–5.
37 DCMS 2004a, 5.
38 DCMS 2004a, 11.
39 Rahman 1995.
40 Matarasso 1997.
41 The most recent Index, published in 2004, considers seven areas: income; employment; health and disability; education, skills and training; housing and services; crime; and the living environment. See Office of the Deputy Prime Minister 2004.
42 For an example of the different ways deprivation can be measured see the study in Northern Ireland Assembly 2003.
43 Indeed, some Government websites provide a 'jargon buster' link (usually very brief) to explain terminology to website users.
44 Such as the conference held by the Department of Museum Studies, Leicester, in 1998. It was also taken up by the Irish Museums Association conference in 2001.
45 A number of these are listed in the bibliography. See for instance: GLLAM 2000; DCMS 2000; RCMG 2001; Parker *et al.* 2002.
46 Each Library and Archive Council in the UK has issued its social inclusion strategy. See for instance that published by the South East Museum, Library and Archive Council 2005–7 available at www.semlac.co.uk.
47 Appleton 2001.
48 Definition provided in DCMS 2004a, 8.
49 Social Exclusion Unit 1998, para. 10.
50 Social Exclusion Unit 1998.
51 Social Exclusion Unit 1998.
52 The approach is explained at www.neighbourhood.gov.uk/, accessed 30 March 2006.
53 Office of the Deputy Prime Minister 2005a.
54 Social Exclusion Unit 1998, paras. 5.29–5.30.
55 Social Exclusion Unit 1998, para. 5.30.
56 Newman and McLean 2002.
57 DCMS 2000.
58 DCMS 2001.
59 DCMS 2001, 10–11.
60 Parker *et al.* 2002; RCMG 2002.
61 GLLAM 2000, 13.
62 GLLAM 2000, 18.
63 GLLAM 2000, 54.
64 GLLAM 2000, 9.
65 Sandell 1998.

66 Scottish Museums Council 2000, 3.
67 Scottish Museums Council 2005, 6.
68 Mark O'Neill, Head of Arts and Museums, Glasgow City Council, email correspondence, 'Social inclusion in Scotland', 29 August 2006.
69 National Museum of Scotland 2002–3; 2003–4; 2005–9.
70 Scottish Executive, 2002.
71 Ruiz 2004, 2.
72 DCAL 2001.
73 Office of the First Minister and Deputy First Minister 2003.
74 The DCAL TSN Plan (DCAL 2004–5; 2005–6) is available at www.dcalni.gov.uk/ContMan/includes/upload/file.asp?ContentID=454&file=c_23.
75 I would like to thank Chris Bailey, Director of Northern Ireland Museums Council, for his thoughtful comments on this subject.
76 Dinham 2005, 304–5.
77 Hoban and Beresford 2001.
78 Hoban and Beresford 2001, 314 (quoting from Home Office (1999) *Report of the Policy Action Team on Community Self-Help*, Active Community Unit, Home Office, London, UK).
79 Hoban and Beresford 2001, 314 (quoting from DETR (2000) *National Strategy for Neighbourhood Renewal*, Report of Policy Action Team 4: Neighbourhood Management, Department of the Environment, Transport and the Regions, London, UK, page 1).
80 Mowbray 2005, 255.
81 Mowbray 2005, 256.
82 Mowbray 2005, 256. See Department for Victorian Communities website: www.dvc.vic.gov.au, accessed 31 August 2005.
83 Mowbray 2005, 257.
84 Mowbray 2005, 257.
85 Marinetto 2003, 114–17.
86 Fremeaux 2005, 268.
87 Fremeaux 2005, 270.
88 Schofield 2002.
89 See their website www.insituteofideas.com.
90 Brighton 2003, 18.
91 Brighton 2003, 19.
92 Newman and McLean 2004a.
93 Newman and McLean 2004a, 174.

4 Social capital and the cultural sector

1 For more information about this group see www.ksg.harvard.edu/saguaro/index.htm.
2 The idea is thought to have originated with Alexis de Tocqueville, who published *Democracy in America* in 1831. See Navarro (2002) for a brief introduction to Tocqueville and Foley.
3 Analysis of the idea is provided in Schuller, Baron and Field 2000.
4 For investigations of these various notions, and how they have been employed in the policy framework, see *Community Development Journal* (Oxford University Press).
5 Bourdieu 1997.
6 Coleman 1988.
7 Bourdieu 1997, 51.
8 This is the subject of an ESRC project Cultural Capital and Social Exclusion: A Critical Investigation, undertaken by Centre for Research on Socio-Cultural Change (CRESC), The University of Manchester. See www.cresc.ac.uk.

9 Putnam 2001.
10 Campbell 2000, 183.
11 Diamond 2004.
12 Munn 2000.
13 MacGillivray and Walker 2000.
14 Phillips 2004.
15 Kay 2000.
16 Carey and Sutton 2004.
17 Saguaro Seminar 2000, 3.
18 Saguaro Seminar 2000, 30.
19 Saguaro Seminar 2000, 33–6.
20 Sharrock, 2006.
21 Gould 2001.
22 Burdett 2004, 2.
23 Daly 2005.
24 Gould 2001.
25 Keaney 2006, particularly Chapters 3 and 5.
26 Newman and McLean 2004b, 491.
27 Newman and McLean 2004b, 494.
28 Stanford 1995.
29 Foley and Edwards 1997, 550.
30 Kay 2005, 170.
31 Campbell 2000, 192.
32 Campbell 2000, 194.
33 Navarro 2002, 427.
34 Navarro 2002, 430.
35 DeFilippis 2001.
36 DeFilippis 2001, 793.
37 Foley and Edwards 1999.
38 DeFilippis 2001, 782.
39 Sharrock 2006.
40 Gould 2001, 70.
41 Bezzina 2006.
42 Gould 2001, 71.
43 For a detailed discussion of one such march, the history of parades, and community relations issues raised by them, see Dingley 2002.
44 American Association of Museums 2005.
45 Casagrande in American Association of Museums 2002a, ix.
46 American Association of Museums 1995, 7.
47 Robert Archibald, 'Rationale for Museums and Community Initiative', www.aam-us.org/initiatives/m&c/papers/rationale.cfm, accessed 25 April 2003.
48 Gates 2002, 23.
49 Robert Archibald, 'Rationale for Museums and Community Initiative', www.aam-us.org/initiatives/m&c/papers/rationale.cfm accessed 25 April 2003.
50 Igoe and Roosa 2002.
51 Museum and Community Initiative Community dialogues, www.aam-us.org/initiatives/m&c/dialogues/index.cfm, accessed 25 April 2003.
52 Community Dialogue, Providence Rhode Island, 20–21 July 2000, www.aam-us.org/initiatives/m&c/dialogues/mciprovidence.cfm, accessed 25 April 2003.
53 Community Dialogue, Los Angeles, 11–12 December 2000, www.aam-us.org/initiatives/m&c/dialogues/mcilosangeles.cfm, accessed 25 April 2003.
54 Community Dialogue, Tampa, Florida, 16–17 November 2000, www.aam-us.org/initiatives/m&c/dialogues/mcilosangeles.cfm, accessed 25 April 2003.

55 AAM Board of Directors Museums and Community Resolution, www.aam-us.org/initiatives/m&c/resoulation.cfm, accessed 25 April 2003.
56 Community Dialogue, Los Angeles, 11–12 December 2000, www.aam-us.org/initiatives/m&c/dialogues/mcilosangeles.cfm, accessed 25 April 2003, and Bellingham, Washington, 21 April 2001 2000, www.aam-us.org/initiatives/m&c/dialogues/bellingham.cfm, accessed 25 April 2003.
57 Community Dialogue, Providence Rhode Island, 20–21 July 2000, www.aam-us.org/initiatives/m&c/dialogues/mciprovidence.cfm, accessed 25 April 2003.
58 Archibald 2002, 5.
59 Hirzy 2002, 15.
60 Hirzy 2002, 10–11.
61 Keaney 2006, 35.

5 Museums, cultural diversity and multiculturalism

1 ICOM 1997, *http://icom.museum/diversity.html*.
2 Such as Malik 1996.
3 Young 2005.
4 UNESCO 2002.
5 UNESCO 2005.
6 UNESCO 2005.
7 Extracts from UNESCO Universal Declaration on Cultural Diversity. Available at www.unesco.org/culture/pluralism/diversity, accessed 18 February 2003.
8 Barry 2001, 328.
9 Barry 2001, Chapter 7.
10 West 2005. This quote was taken from West's essay, of the same title, available on www.spiked-online.com/index.php?/site/printable/684/, accessed 31 July 2006.
11 See opening pages of West 2005.
12 See, for instance, his address to the Institute of Ideas and Institut Français meeting 'Attention Seeking: Multiculturalism and the Politics of Recognition'. Session: Can multiculturalism work? 16 November 2002. Transcript available at www.instituteofideas.com, accessed 31 July 2006.
13 Malik 1996, 177.
14 Dembour 1996.
15 Dembour 1996, 24.
16 Glendon 1991, xi.
17 Figueiredo 2003.
18 Naseem Khan's response can also be found at www.spiked-online.com/Articles/00000006DDD8.htm.
19 Khan 2002, 4. Other information from throughout the report.
20 Verma 2003.
21 Graves 2003.
22 Jenkins 2003.
23 Khan 2003.
24 Somers Cocks 2003.
25 Young 2005.
26 Museums Australia 2000.
27 Khan 2000.
28 Khan 2000.
29 North West Museums Service *et al.* 2002.
30 More information on the Diversify Scheme available at www.museumsassociation.org. An evaluation of the scheme is provided in Shaw 2004.
31 Race Relations Act 1976 (section 38).

32 As stated on the website of the Commission for Racial Equality, www.cre.gov.uk/legal/rra_positive.html, accessed 26 October 2006.
33 Porter 2004, 13.
34 For further information see www.museumoflondon.org.uk/English/Collections/Online Resources/RWWC/About/, accessed 11 August 2006.
35 For further information see www.museumoflondon.org.uk/English/Collections/Online Resources/RWWC/About/, accessed 11 August 2006.
36 Kaur 2005.
37 Chris Bailey, personal communication, 23 October 2006.
38 Morrow 2004, 3.
39 Fraser 2004, 2.
40 Donegan 2006.
41 Bronagh Cleary, Development Officer, Fermanagh County Museum, personal communication, 23 October 2006.
42 Taylor 1994.
43 Taylor 1994, 26.
44 Taylor 1994, 64.
45 The brochure for the course states that the majority of bursaries will be awarded to South African Affirmative Action candidates, see www.robben-island.org.za.
46 As described on the website www.labour.gov.za, accessed 31 October 2006.
47 Davison 1993.
48 Davison 1993, 168–9.
49 Davison 1993, 169.
50 Davison 1993, 178.
51 Lohman 2001.
52 TV coverage March 2001.
53 Gosling 2001.
54 Naidoo 2006.

6 Museums and community relations in Northern Ireland

1 In Northern Ireland the use of language is often very politically loaded. For some the words 'conflict' or 'Troubles' would not fully represent the period; others might prefer the term 'war' or 'struggle'. In addition, the terms Northern Ireland, Ulster, six counties, province and North of Ireland each have different connotations. In this study I will refer to the Troubles and Northern Ireland.
2 Morrissey *et al.* 1999.
3 Hughes and Donnelly 2001, 4; see also Hughes and Donnelly 2004.
4 For an explanation of current community relations work of the Community Relations Council in Northern Ireland see www.community-relations.org.uk.
5 Finlay 2004.
6 Personal communication with Madeline McCreevy, Ulster Folk and Transport Museum, 8 August 2006.
7 Personal communication with Madeline McCreevy, Ulster Folk and Transport Museum, 8 August 2006.
8 McVeigh 2002.
9 Rolston 1998.
10 Buckley and Kenny 1994, 131.
11 Buckley and Kenny 1994, 131.
12 Jane Leonard, personal communication, 2001.
13 Linda McKenna, personal communication, 2003.
14 Down County Museum 2003.
15 Smith and Robinson 1992; 1996; Richardson 1997.

16 Smith and Robinson 1992, 13.
17 Buckley and Kenny 1994.
18 Department of Education 2005.
19 O'Connor, Hartop and McCully 2002.
20 Madeline McGreevy, Community Relations Officer, UFTM, personal communication via email, 11 August 2006.
21 Department of Education 2005, 3.
22 Northern Ireland Schools Community Relations Programme, 'Developing Community Relations Practice', available at www.creni.org/contents/developing_community_relations_practice.
23 Madeline McGreevy, Community Relations Officer, UFTM, personal communication via email, 11 August 2006.
24 Statement taken from Ulster Folk and Transport Museum website www.uftm.org.uk/learning/Community_Relations, accessed on 10 July 2006.
25 Madeline McGreevy, Community Relations Officer, UFTM, personal communication via email, 11 August 2006.
26 An Orange Hall is a building associated with Protestant people. It would have been erected by the Orange Order and used for their meetings. In addition, local Protestant families, schools and churches would use the building for events such as concerts and indoor sports.
27 Quote taken from leaflet for Leck House workshop, August 2006.
28 Facilitator notes, Leck House workshop (courtesy of Madeline McGreevy, August 2006).
29 Pupil evaluation, Leck House Workshop, 16 November 2005 (courtesy of Madeline McGreevy, August 2006).
30 Pupil evaluation, Leck House Workshop, 16 November 2005; Community Relations evaluation, UFTM Education Department, various dates in 2006 (courtesy of Madeline McGreevy, August 2006).
31 Student evaluation of a workshop exploring identity, 10 November 2005 (courtesy of Madeline McGreevy, August 2006) and feedback report to schools written by Rachel Osbourne, Education Assistant.
32 Morrissey *et al.* 1999.
33 Northern Ireland Statistics and Research Agency 2005.
34 Lacey 1993, 57.
35 Lacey 1993; 1994.
36 For a detailed description of the exhibition, and useful analysis, see Bell 1998.
37 *Newsletter*, December 1996, *The Times*, 26 December 1996, and *The Sentinel*, 10 September 1992 and 30 July 1992.
38 Bell 1998, 23.
39 Lacey 1994.
40 Quotes taken from Museums Community Relations Training, monitoring and evaluation summary of results (Tower Museum 2004–5).
41 Office of the First Minister and Deputy First Minister 2005, 7.
42 Office of the First Minister and Deputy First Minister 2005, 10.
43 Office of the First Minister and Deputy First Minister 2005, 33.
44 Office of the First Minister and Deputy First Minister, 2006.
45 Chris Bailey, Director Northern Ireland Museums Council, personal communication, 29 September 2006.
46 Longley 2001, 41.
47 Smith and Robinson 1996, 77.
48 Smith and Robinson 1996, 78.
49 Barton and McCully 2005.
50 Barton and McCully 2003; 2005, 108.

7 Museums and community movements

1 Lovett 1995, 279.
2 Falls Community Council 2001, 4.
3 Blumer 1951.
4 Lovett 1995, 280.
5 Mayo 1995.
6 Lovett 1995, 284.
7 Ulster People's College 2002.
8 Office of the Minister and Deputy First Minister 2005.
9 Shared Future – a response from Ulster People's College, 30 September 2003; see www.asharedfutureni.gov.uk.
10 Ulster People's College 2002.
11 Lovett 1995, 284.
12 Ulster People's College 2002, 2.
13 Ulster People's College 2002, 6.
14 Mayo 1999, 146–50.
15 Karen McCartney, Lecturer in Adult and Community Education, Ulster People's College, personal communication, November 2005.
16 Ulster People's College, Project Report, July 2003–December 2003.
17 Ulster People's College 2002.
18 Ulster People's College 2002.
19 Ulster People's College, Project Report, July 2003–December 2003, Community Relations Council EU Programme for Peace and Reconciliation Measure 2.1 Reconciliation for Sustainable Peace (no page numbers). Similar findings also recorded in reports for the following periods: September 2002–June 2003; January 2004–June 2004; July 2004–December 2004; January 2005–June 2005.
20 Report for period January 2005–June 2005.
21 Ulster People's College/People's History Initiative, Project Report, September 2002–June 2003.
22 Ulster People's College/People's History Initiative, Project Report, July 2003–December 2003.
23 Ulster People's College/People's History Initiative, Project Report, July 2003–December 2003.
24 Ulster People's College/People's History Initiative, Project Report, July 2003–December 2003.
25 Information on the calculation of this index is available at www.nisra.gov.uk. For interpretation of the index consult Beatty 2004.
26 My thanks go to Oliver Casey, Greater Linenhall Area Heritage Committee, for a personal tour of the exhibition on the opening night, 1 July 2003.
27 District Six Museum mission statement taken from the museum website www.districtsix.co.za, accessed on 6 March 2001
28 Fredericks 2001, 13–14.
29 Abrahams 2001, 4.
30 Le Grange 2001, 7.
31 Fredericks 2001, 14.
32 Soudien 2001, 5–6.
33 Prosalendis *et al.* 77.
34 Rassool 2001, x.
35 S. Prosalendis, personal communication, Cape Town, 5 April 2001.
36 S. Prosalendis, personal communication, Cape Town, 5 April 2001.
37 S. Prosalendis, personal communication, Cape Town, 5 April 2001.
38 Rassool 2001a, viii.
39 Le Grange 2001, 7.

40 Kolbe 2001, 15.
41 Combrinck 2001, 9.
42 Kolbe 2001, 15.
43 Soudien 2001, 5.
44 Le Grange 2001, 7.
45 Rassool 2000.
46 Rassool 2006.
47 Rassool 2006, 17.
48 Falls Community Council 2001, 6.
49 Falls Community Council 2001.
50 Martin 2004, 29.
51 Falls Community Council 2001, 12.
52 Dillon and Taillon 1997.
53 www.ohs.org.uk/#whatisoh, accessed 16 September 2005.
54 Falls Community Council 2001, 19–21.
55 Falls Community Council 2001, 15.
56 Falls Community Council 2001, 7.
57 C. Hackett, personal communication, 11 October 2002.
58 Hackett 2003.
59 Falls Community Council 2001, 19.
60 House of Commons Northern Ireland Affairs Select Committee, *Ways of Dealing with Northern Ireland's Past: Interim Report Tenth Report of Session 2004–5*. Victims and Survivors (April 2005), London: The Stationery Office, Ref: HC303–1. In particular see: Written Evidence Falls Community Council Ev. 325.
61 Hackett 2003.
62 Hackett 2003.
63 Hackett 2003.
64 www.bloodysundaytrust.org, accessed 26 September 2006.
65 www.museumoffreederry.org, accessed 26 September 2006.
66 Bauman 2001.
67 Brent 1997, 68–83.
68 Cohen 1985, 101.

Conclusion

1 Wood and Gould 2005, 2.
2 Wood and Gould 2005, 12.
3 Wood and Gould 2005, 17.
4 Wood and Gould 2005, 2.
5 Fraser 2005.
6 Such as the exhibition Sexwise at Nottingham Castle and Art Gallery, May 2000, delivered in association with Nottingham Health Authority.
7 Rassool 2006, 14.
8 Edwards 2001 in Peers and Brown 2003, 5.
9 Clifford 1997, 192.
10 Such as the commemoration of the bicentenary of the 1798 Rebellion and, to a lesser extent, the 150th anniversary of the 1840s Famine.
11 I am thinking here of the proposal to develop part of the Maze Prison as a museum; the Museum of Free Derry, which has recently opened with minimum resources and services; the investigations into a museum of the Troubles, led by Healing Through Remembering and, finally, the proposal to develop a museum coming from Falls Community Council.

12 Comments from Mark O'Neill, Head of Arts and Museums, email correspondence 'Social Inclusion Scotland', 5 October 2006.
13 Jowell 2006.
14 Heartfield 2005.
15 Clifford 1997, 192.

Bibliography

Abrahams, S. (2001) 'A Place of Sanctuary' in Rassool and Prosalendis 2001, 3–4.

Adams, R. (2003) *Social Work and Empowerment*. New York, Palgrave Macmillan.

American Association of Museums (1995) *Museums in the Life of a City: Strategies for Community Partnerships*. Washington, DC, AAM.

—— (2002a) *Mastering Civic Engagement: A Challenge to Museums*. Washington, DC, AAM.

—— (2002b) *Museums and Community Toolkit*. Washington, DC, AAM.

—— (2005) *Annual Report 2005*. Washington, DC, AAM.

Amit, V. (ed.) (2002) *Realizing Community: Concepts, Social Relationships and Sentiments*. London, Routledge.

Anderson, B. (1991) *Imagined Communities: Reflections on the Origin and Spread of Nationalism*. London, Verso.

Appleton, J. (2001) *Museums for the People? Conversations in Print*. London, Institute of Ideas.

Archibald, R. (2002) 'Introduction' in American Association of Museums 2002a, 1–8.

Baron, S., J. Field and T. Schuller (eds.) (2000) *Social Capital: Critical Perspectives*. Oxford, Oxford University Press.

Barry, B. (2001) *Culture and Equality: An Egalitarian Critique of Multiculturalism*. Cambridge, Polity Press.

Barton, K. C. and A. W. McCully (2003) 'History Teaching and the Perpetuation of Memories: The Northern Ireland Experience' in E. Cairns and M. D. Roe (eds.), *The Role of Memory in Ethnic Conflict*. Basingstoke, Palgrave Macmillan, 107–43.

—— (2005) 'History, Identity and the School Curriculum in Northern Ireland: An Empirical Study of Secondary Students' Ideas and Perspectives'. *Journal of Curriculum Studies* 37 (1), 85–116.

Bauman, Z. (2001) *Community Seeking Safety in an Insecure World*. London, Polity Press.

Beatty, R. (2004) *Northern Ireland Multiple Deprivation Measure: A Users Guide*. Belfast, Northern Ireland Statistics Research Agency.

Bell, D. (1998) 'Modernising History: The Real Politik of Heritage and Cultural Traditions in Northern Ireland' in D. Miller (ed.), *Rethinking Northern Ireland*. Harlow, Longman, 228–52.

Bennett, T. (1995) *The Birth of the Museum*. London, Routledge.

Bezzina, H. (2006) 'Community, Government and Museum – the *Peranakan* of Singapore', Paper presented at Museums Australia National Conference *Exploring Dynamics Cities, Cultural Spaces, Communities*. Available at www.museumsaustralia.org, accessed 7 June 2006.

Blumer, H. (1951) 'Social Movements', reprinted in S. M. Lyman (ed.), *Social Movements: Critiques, Concepts, Case Studies*. London and Basingstoke, Macmillan, 1995, 60–81.

Bourdieu, P. (1997) 'Forms of Capital' in A. H. Halsey, H. Lauder, P. Brown and A. S. Wells (eds.), *Education, Culture, Economy, Society*. Oxford, Oxford University Press, 46–58.

Brent, J. (1997) 'Community without Unity' in Hoggett 1997, 68–83.

Brighton, A. (2003) 'Save our Souls'. *Museum Journal*, 103 (7), 18–19.

Brow, J. (1990) 'Notes on Community, Hegemony, and the Uses of the Past'. *Anthropological Quarterly* 63 (1), 1–6.

Buckley, A. and M. Kenny (1994) 'Cultural Heritage in an Oasis of Calm: Divided Identities in a Museum in Ulster' in U. Kockel (ed.), *Culture Tourism and Development: The Case of Ireland*. Liverpool, Liverpool University Press, 65–73.

Burdett, R. (2004) *Museums and Galleries: Creative Engagement*. London: National Museums Directors' Conference.

Butcher, H. (1993) 'Introduction: Some Examples and Definitions' in Butcher *et al.* 1993, 3–21.

Butcher, H., A. Glen, P. Henderson and J. Smith (1993) *Community and Public Policy*. London, Pluto Press.

Campbell, C. (2000) 'Social Capital and Health: Contextualizing Health Promotion within Local Community Networks' in Baron *et al.* 2000, 182–96.

Campfens, H. (ed.) (1997) *Community Development around the World: Practice, Theory, Research, Training*. Toronto, University of Toronto Press.

Carbonell, B. M. (ed.) (2004) *Museum Studies: An Anthology of Contexts*. Oxford, Blackwell.

Carey, P. and S. Sutton (2004) 'Community Development through Participatory Arts: Lessons Learned from a Community Arts and Regeneration Project in Southern Liverpool'. *Community Development Journal* 39 (2), 123–34.

Carter, J. C. (1992) 'Escaping the Bounds: Putting Community Back into Museums'. *Muse* 10 (2/3), 61–2.

Clifford, J. (1997) *Routes: Travel and Translation in the Late Twentieth Century*. Cambridge, MA, Harvard University Press.

Cochrane, A. (1986) 'Community Politics and Democracy' in D. Held and C. Pollitt (eds.), *New Forms of Democracy*. London, Sage, 51–75.

Cohen, A. (1985) *The Symbolic Construction of Community*. London and New York, Tavistock.

Coleman, J. (1988) 'Social Capital in the Creation of Human Capital', reprinted in A. H. Halsey, H. Lauder, P. Brown and A. S. Wells (eds.), *Education, Culture, Economy, Society*. Oxford, Oxford University Press, 1997, 80–95.

Combrinck, I. (2001) 'A museum of consciousness' in Rassool and Prosalendis 2001, 9–10.

Corsane, G. (ed.) (2005) *Heritage, Museums and Galleries: An Introductory Reader*. London, Routledge.

Craig, G. and M. Mayo (eds.) (1995) *Community Empowerment: A Reader in Participation and Development*. London, Zed Books.

Crooke, E. (2000) *Politics, Archaeology and the Creation of a National Museum of Ireland: An Expression of National Life*. Dublin, Irish Academic Press.

Daly, S. (2005) *Social Capital and the Cultural Sector: Literature Review Prepared for DCMS*. London, Centre for Civil Society, London School of Economics.

Davalos, K. M. (1998) 'Exhibiting Mestizaje: The Poetics and Experience of the Mexican Fine Arts Center Museum', reprinted in Carbonell 2004, 522–37.

Davis, P. (2005) 'Places, "Cultural Touchstones" and the Ecomuseum' in Corsane 2005, 365–76.

Davison, P. (1993) 'Human Subjects as Museum Objects. A Project to Make Life-casts of "Bushmen" and "Hottentots", 1907–1924'. *Annals of the South African Museum* 102 (5), 165–83.

Dawson, A. (2002) 'The Mining Community and the Ageing Body: Towards a Phenomenology of Community?' in Amit 2002, 21–37.

Dean, D. (1994) *Museum Exhibition: Theory and Practice*. London, Routledge.

DeFilippis, J. (2001) 'The Myth of Social Capital in Community Development'. *Housing Policy Debate* 12 (4), 781–806.

Delanty, G. (2003) *Community*. London, Routledge.

Dembour, M. (1996) 'Human Rights Talk and Anthropological Ambivalence. The

Particular Contexts of Universal Claims' in O. Harris (ed.), *Inside and Outside the Law: Anthropological Studies of Authority and Ambiguity*. London, Routledge, 19–40.

Denham, J. (2001) *Building Cohesive Communities: A Report of the Ministerial Group on Public Order and Community Cohesion*. London, Home Office.

Department of Culture, Arts and Leisure (2001) *Corporate Strategy, 2001–2004*. Belfast, DCAL.

—— (2004–5) *New Targeting Social Need Action Plan*. Belfast, DCAL.

—— (2005–6) *New Targeting Social Need Action Plan*. Belfast, DCAL.

Department of Culture, Media and Sport (2000) *Centres for Social Change: Museums, Galleries and Libraries for All*. London, DCMS.

—— (2001) *Libraries, Museums, Galleries and Archives for all*. London, DCMS.

—— (2004a) *Culture at the Heart of Regeneration*. London, DCMS.

—— (2004b) *Bringing Communities together through Sport and Culture*. Oldham, DCMS, Oldham. Available at: www.culture.gov.uk/NR/rdonlyres/5CE87526–274F–4671–8FC5–0D62F9B1C186/0/CommunitiesBooklet.pdf.

Department of Education (2005) *Schools' Community Relations Programme: Guidelines for Schools*. Belfast: The Northern Ireland Education and Library Boards.

Diamond, J. (2004) 'Local Regeneration Initiatives and Capacity Building: Whose "Capacity" and "Building" for What?' *Community Development Journal* 39 (2), 177–89.

Díaz-Andreu, M. and T. Champion (eds.) (1996) *Nationalism and Archaeology in Europe*. London, Routledge.

Dillon, B. and R. Taillon (1997) *Feasibility Study into the Establishment of a Community Archive*. Dublin, Falls Community Council and Nexus.

Dingley, J. (2002) 'Marching Down the Garvaghy Road: Republican Tactics and State Response to the Orangemen's Claim to March their Traditional Route Home after the Drumcree Church Service'. *Terrorism and Political Violence* 14 (3), 42–79.

Dinham, A. (2005) 'Empowered or Over-powered? The Real Experiences of Local Participation in the UK's New Deal for Communities'. *Community Development Journal* 40 (3), 301–12.

Donegan, C. (2006) 'Welcoming Diversity'. *Impartial Reporter* 17 August.

Down County Museum (2003) *The Bicentenary of the 1803 Rebellion Events* [pamphlet]. Downpatrick, Down County Museum.

Evans, K. (1997) ' "It's all right 'round here if you're a local": Community in the Inner City' in Hoggett 1997, 33–50.

Falls Community Council (2001) *Engaging with Change Falls Community Council Development Plan 2001–6*. Belfast, Falls Community Council.

Figueiredo, D. (2003) 'Is Cultural Diversity Policy Good for the Arts? Yes'. *Spiked* 9 June.

Finlay, A. (ed.) (2004) *Nationalism and Multiculturalism: Irish Identity, Citizenship and the Peace Process*. London, Transaction.

Foley, M. W. and B. Edwards (1997) 'Escape from Politics? Social Theory and the Social Capital Debate'. *American Behavioral Scientist* 40 (5), 550–61.

—— (1999) 'Is It Time To Disinvest in Social Capital?' *Journal of Public Policy* 19 (2), 141–73.

Fraser, H. (2005) 'Four Different Approaches to Community Participation'. *Community Development Journal* 40 (3), 285–300.

Fraser, T. (2004) 'Foreword' in Northern Ireland Museums Council 2004, 2.

Fredericks, T. (2001) 'Creating the District Six Museum' in Rassool and Prosalendis 2001, 13–14.

Freire, P. (1972) *Pedagogy of the Oppressed*. London, Penguin.

Fremeaux, I. (2005) 'New Labour's Appropriation of the Concept of Community: A Critique'. *Community Development Journal* 40 (3), 265–74.

Gates, G. T. (2002) 'The Civic Landscape' in American Association of Museums 2002a, 23–8.

Gilchrist, A. and M. Taylor (1997) 'Community Networking: Developing Strength through Diversity' in Hoggett 1997, 165–79.

Glendon, M. A. (1991) *Rights Talk: The Improverishment of Political Discourse*. New York, The Free Press, Macmillan.

GLLAM (2000) *Museums and Social Inclusion: The GLLAM Report*. Leicester: Research Centre for Museums and Galleries.

Gosling, M. (2001) 'San shocked at closure of exhibit'. *Cape Times* 30 March, 1.

Gould, H. (2001) 'Culture and Social Capital' in F. Matarasso (ed.), *Recognising Culture: A Series of Briefing Papers on Culture and Development*. Cheltenham: Comedia, Department of Canadian Heritage and UNESCO, 69–75.

Graves, T. (2003) 'Is Cultural Diversity Good for the Arts? Deepening Diversity'. *Spiked* 13 June.

Gray, J. (2002) 'Community as Place Making: Ram Auctions in the Scottish Borderland', in Amit 2002, 38–59.

Hackett, C. (2003) 'Creative Activity for Everyone'. *Contexts* Spring.

Healy, K. (2003) 'Mobilizing Community Museum Networks in Mexico and Beyond'. *Grassroots Development: Journal of the Inter-American Foundation* 24 (1), 15–24.

Heartfield, J. (2005) 'Abolish the DCMS'. *Spiked* 17 May.

Hirzy, E. (2002) 'Mastering Civic Engagement: A Report from the American Association of Museums' in American Association of Museums 2002a, 9–22.

Hoban, M. and P. Beresford (2001) 'Regenerating Regeneration'. *Community Development Journal* 36 (4), 312–20.

Hoggett, P. (ed.) (1997) *Contested Communities: Experiences, Struggles, Policies*. Bristol, The Policy Press.

Home Office (2004) *Confident Communities in a Secure Britain: The Home Office Strategic Plan 2004–8*. London, Home Office.

Hooper-Greenhill, E. (2000) *Museums and the Interpretation of Visual Culture*. London, Routledge.

House of Commons (2005) *Hansard*. Written Answers for 2 March 2005 Column 1204W.

Howell, S. (2002) 'Community beyond Place: Adoptive Families in Norway' in Amit 2002, 84–104.

Hughes, J. and C. Donnelly (2001) *Ten Years of Social Attitudes to Community Relations in Northern Ireland*. Northern Ireland Life and Times Survey Occasional Paper 1, School of Policy Studies, University of Ulster.

—— (2004) 'Attitudes to Community Relations in Northern Ireland: Signs of Optimism in the Post Cease-Fire Period?' *Terrorism and Political Violence* 16 (3), 567–92.

ICOM (1997) *Museums and Cultural Diversity: Policy Statement*. Paris, ICOM.

—— (2006) *Code of Ethics for Museums*. Paris, ICOM.

Igoe, K. and A. M. Roosa (2002) 'Listening to the Voices of Our Communities'. *Journal of Museum Education* 27 (2&3), 16–21.

James, P. (2001) 'Building a Community-based Identity at Anacostia Museum', reprinted in Corsane 2005, 339–56.

Jenkins, T. (2003) 'Is Cultural Diversity Good for the Arts? A Formula for Indifference'. *Spiked* 13 June.

Jones, S. (2005) 'Making Place, Revisiting Displacement: Conflicting National and Local Identities in Scotland' in Littler and Naidoo 2005, 94–114.

Jowell, T. (2006) Keynote Speech at the 'Capturing the Value of Heritage' event at the Royal Geographical Society, London.

Kaplan, F. E. S. (ed.) (1994) *Museums and the Making of Ourselves: The Role of Objects in National Identity*. Leicester, Leicester University Press.

Karp, I. (1992) 'Introduction: Museums and Communities: The Politics of Public Culture' in Karp *et al.* 1992, 1–17.

Karp, I., C. M. Kreamer and S. D. Lavine (eds.) (1992) *Museums and Communities: The Politics of Public Culture*. London and Washington, DC, Smithsonian Institution Press.

Kaur, R. (2005) *Unearthing Our Past: Engaging with Diversity at the Museum of London*. London, Museum of London.

Kay, A. (2000) 'Art and Community Development: The Role the Arts Have in Regenerating Communities'. *Community Development Journal* 35 (4), 414–24.

—— (2005) 'Social Capital, the Social Economy and Community Development'. *Community Development Journal* 41 (2), 160–73.

Keaney, E. (2006) *Cultural Policy and Civic Renewal*. London, Institute of Public Policy Research.

Kelly, L. (2005) 'Evaluation, Research and Communities of Practice: Program Evaluation in Museums'. *Archival Science* 4, 35–69.

Kelly, L. and P. Gordon (2002) 'Developing a community of practice: museums and reconciliation in Australia' in Sandell 2002, 153–74.

Khan, N. (2000) *Responding to Cultural Diversity: Guidance for Museums and Galleries Fact Sheet*. London, Museums and Galleries Commission.

—— (2002) *Towards a Greater Diversity: Results of the Arts Council of England's Cultural Diversity Action Plan*. London, The Arts Council of England.

—— (2003) 'Is Cultural Diversity Policy Good for the Arts? Change the Whole Agenda'. *Spiked* 9 July.

Kolbe, V. (2001) 'Museum beginnings' in Rassool and Prosalendis 2001, 15–16.

Lacey, B. (1993) 'The Derry Museum Service and the Regeneration of the City'. *Museum Ireland* 3, 57–63.

—— (1994) 'Untangling the Knots of Myth and History – Developing a Museum Service for Derry'. *Causeway* 1 (4), 27–30.

Le Grange, L. (2001) 'The Collective Spirit of a Museum' in Rassool and Prosalendis 2001, 7–8.

Leicestershire County Council Community Services (2004) *Community Museums Strategy 2004–2009*. Leicester, Leicestershire County Council.

Lev-Wiesel, R. (2003) 'Indicators Constituting the Construct of "Perceived Community Cohesion" '. *Community Development Journal* 38 (4), 332–43.

Linley, R. (2004) *New Directions in Social Policy: Communities and Inclusion Policy for Museums, Libraries and Archives*. London, Museums, Libraries and Archives Council.

Littler, J. and R. Naidoo (eds.) (2005) *The Politics of Heritage: The Legacies of 'Race'*. London, Routledge.

Local Government Association (2004) *Community Cohesion – An Action Guide: Guidance for Local Authorities*. London, Local Government Association.

Lohman, J. (2001) Press speech at the closing of the Bushman Diorama, 3 April 2001. Iziko Museums of Cape Town.

Longley, E. (2001) 'Multiculturalism and Northern Ireland: Making Differences Fruitful' in E. Longley and D. Kiberd (eds.), *Multi-culturalism: The View from the Two Irelands*. Cork, Cork University Press, 1–44.

Lovett, T. (1995) 'Popular Education in Northern Ireland: The Ulster People's College' in Mayo and Thompson 1995, 257–86.

Lowe, S. S. 2000 'Creating Community. Art for Community Development'. *Journal of Contemporary Ethnography* 29 (3), 357–86.

Lyman, S. M. (ed.) (1995) *Social Movements: Critiques, Concepts, Case Studies*. London and Basingstoke, Macmillan.

MacGillivray, A. and P. Walker (2000) 'Local Social Capital: Making it Work on the Ground' in S. Baron *et al.*, 197–211.

Malik, K. (1996) *The Meaning of Race*. London, Macmillan.

Marinetto, M. (2003) 'Who Wants To Be an Active Citizen? The Politics and Practice of Community Involvement'. *Sociology* 37 (1), 103–20.

Martin, G. (2004) 'New Social Movements and Democracy' in Todd and Taylor 2004, 29–54.

Mason, R. (2004) 'Conflict and Complement: An Exploration of the Discourses Informing the Concept of the Socially Inclusive Museum in Contemporary Britain'. *International Journal of Heritage Studies* 10 (1), 49–73.

—— (2005) 'Museums, Galleries and Heritage: Sites of Meaning-making and Communication', in Corsane 2005, 200–14.

Matarasso, F. (1997) *Use or Ornament? The Social Impact of Participation in the Arts*. Winchester, Comedia.

Mayo, M. (1995) 'Adult Education for Change in the Nineties and Beyond: Towards a Critical Review of the Changing Context' in Mayo and Thompson 1995, 5–17.

—— (2000) *Cultures, Communities, Identities: Cultural Strategies for Participation and Empowerment*. London, Palgrave.

Mayo, M. and G. Craig (1995) 'Community Participation and Empowerment: The Human Face of Structural Adjustment or Tools for Democratic Transformation?' in Craig and Mayo 1995, 1–11.

Mayo, M. and J. Thompson (eds.) (1995) *Adult Learning, Critical Intelligence and Social Change*. Leicester: NIACE, The National Organisation for Adult Learning.

Mayo, P. (1999) *Gramsci, Freire and Adult Education: Possibilities for Transformative Action*. London and New York, Zed Books.

McVeigh, R. (2002) 'Between Reconciliation and Pacification: The British State and Community Relations in the North of Ireland'. *Community Development Journal* 37 (1), 47–59.

Miller, D. (1998) 'Why Some Things Matter' in D. Miller (ed.), *Material Cultures*. Chicago, University of Chicago Press, 3–21.

Morrissey, M., M. Smyth, M. T. Fay and T. Wong (1999) *The Cost of the Troubles Study. Report on the Northern Ireland Survey: The Experience and Impact of the Troubles*. Londonderry, INCORE, University of Ulster.

Morrow, D. (2004) 'Foreword' in Northern Ireland Museums Council 2004, 3.

Mowbray, M. (2005) 'Community Capacity Building or State Opportunism?' *Community Development Journal* 40 (3), 255–64.

Mpumlwana, K., G. Corsane, J. Pastor-Makhurane and C. Rassool (2002) 'Inclusion and the Power of Representation: South African Museums and the Cultural Politics of Social Transformation' in Sandell 2002, 244–61.

Munn, P. (2000) 'Social Capital, Schools, and Exclusions' in S. Baron *et al.* 2000, 168–81.

Murakami, K. (2005) 'Regeneration of a Community: Development of a Township Museum in the Post-apartheid South Africa'. *Horizontes* 23 (1), 57–65.

Museums Association (2000) *Code of Ethics*. London, Museums Association.

Museums Australia (2000) *Cultural Diversity Policy*. ACT, Museums Australia Incorporated.

Museums, Libraries and Archives Council (2005) *Sustainable Communities Summit Bulletin*. London, MLA.

—— (2003) *Diversity Policy*. London, MLA.

Naidoo, R. (2005) 'Never Mind the Buzzwords: "Race", Heritage and the Liberal Agenda' in Littler and Naidoo 2006, 36–48.

National Council on Archives (2005) *Minutes of the Community Archives Development Group* including: 12 September 2005 and 5 December 2005. Available at www.ncaonline.org.uk.

—— (2006) *Minutes of the Community Archives Development Group* 14 March 2006. Available at www.ncaonline.org.uk.

National Museum of Scotland (2002/3) *Annual Review*. Edinburgh, NMS.

—— (2003/4) *Annual Review*. Edinburgh, NMS.

—— (2005–9) *Corporate Plan*. Edinburgh, NMS.

Navarro, V. (2002) 'A Critique of Social Capital'. *International Journal of Health Services* 32 (3), 423–32.

Neilson, L. C. (2003) 'The Development of Marketing in the Canadian Museum Community, 1840–1989'. *Journal of Macromarketing* 23 (1), 16–30.

Newman, A. and F. McLean (2002) 'Architectures of Social Inclusion: Museums, Galleries and Inclusive Communities' in Sandell 2002, 56–68.

—— (2004a) 'Presumption, Policy and Practice. The Use of Museums and Galleries as Agents of Social Inclusion in Great Britain'. *International Journal of Cultural Policy* 10 (2), 167–81.

—— (2004b) 'Capital and the Evaluation of the Museum Experience'. *International Journal of Cultural Studies* 7 (4), 480–98.

Nightingale, E. and D. Swallow (2003) 'The Arts of the Sikh Kingdoms. Collaborating with a Community' in Peers and Brown 2003, 55–71.

North East Museums, Libraries and Archives Council (2003) *Cultural Diversity Strategy*. Newcastle, North East Museums, Libraries and Archives Council.

North West Museums Service, North Western Regional Library System, North West Regional

Archives Council (2002) *Museums, Archives and Libraries Cultural Diversity Forum Summary of Activity April 2001–March 2002.* Washington, North West Museums Service.

Northern Ireland Assembly (2003) *Measures of Deprivation Noble v. Robson.* Northern Ireland Assembly Research Paper 02/02. Belfast: Research and Library Services, Northern Ireland Assembly.

Northern Ireland Museums Council (2004) *Our People Our Times: A History of Northern Ireland's Cultural Diversity.* Belfast, NIMC.

Northern Ireland Schools Community Relations Programme (no date) 'Developing Community Relations Practice'. Available at www.creni.org/contents/developing_community_relations_practice, accessed August 2006.

Northern Ireland Statistics and Research Agency (2005) *Northern Ireland Multiple Deprivation Index.* Belfast, Northern Ireland Statistics and Research Agency.

O'Connor, U., B. Hartop and A. McCully (2002) *A Review of the Schools Community Relations Programme.* Belfast, Department of Education Northern Ireland.

Office of the Deputy Prime Minister (2004) *The English Indices of Deprivation 2004: Summary (Revised).* London, Office of the Deputy Prime Minister.

—— (2005a) *Research Report 17 New Deal for Communities 2001–2005: An Interim Evaluation Undertaken by Sheffield Hallam University.* London. Available at http://www.neighbourhood.gov.uk/publications.asp?did=1625.

—— (2005b) *Sustainable Communities: People, Places and Prosperity.* Report Presented to Parliament by the Deputy Prime Minster and First Secretary of State by Command of Her Majesty, January 2005 Cm 6425.

Office of the First Minister and Deputy First Minister (2003) *Interim Evaluation of New TSN, Summary and Synthesis Report.* Belfast, Deloitte and Touche.

—— (2005) *A Shared Future: Policy Strategic Framework for Good Relations in Northern Ireland.* Belfast, Community Relations Unit OFMDFM.

—— (2006) *A Shared Future: First Triennial Action Plan 2006–2009.* Belfast, OFMDFM.

Parker, S., K. Waterston, G. Michaluk and L. Rickhard (2002) *Neighbourhood Renewal and Social Inclusion: The Role of Museums, Archives and Libraries.* London, University of Northumbria and London, Re:source.

Peers, L. and A. K. Brown (eds.) (2003) *Museums and Source Communities.* London, Routledge.

Phillips, R. (2004) 'Artful Business: Using the Arts for Community Economic Development'. *Community Development Journal* 39 (2), 112–22.

Porter, G. (2004) *Diversify! The Impact of Positive Action Traineeships.* London, Museums, Libraries and Archives Council.

Putnam, R. D. (2001) *Bowling Alone: The Collapse and Revival of American Community.* London, Touchstone.

Race Relations Act, 1976. London, HMSO.

Rahman, M. A. (1995) 'Participatory Development: Toward Liberation or Co-optation?' in Craig and Mayo 1995, 24–32.

Rassool, C. (2000) Community Museums, Memory Politics and Social Transformations: Histories, Possibilities and Limits. Unpublished manuscript.

—— (2001a) 'Introduction' in Rassool and Prosalendis 2001, 1–4.

—— (2001b) 'Memory and the Politics of History at the District Six Museum'. Paper delivered to the Mapping Alternatives: Debating New Heritage Practices in South Africa workshop, 25–6 September 2001, Centre for African Studies, University of Cape Town.

—— (2006) 'Making the District Six Museum in Cape Town'. *Museum International* 58 (1–2), 9–18.

Rassool, C. and S. Prosalendis (eds.) (2001) *Recalling Community in Cape Town: Creating and Curating the District Six Museum.* Cape Town, District Six Museum.

Research Centre for Museums and Galleries (2001) *Small Museums and Social Inclusion.* Leicester, RCMG.

—— (2002) *A Catalyst for Change: The Social Impact of the Open Museum.* Leicester, RCMG.

Re:source, The Council for Museums, Archives and Libraries (2000) *Manifesto*. London, Re:source.

—— (2001) *Using Museums, Archives and Libraries To Develop a Learning Community: A Strategic Plan for Action*. London, Re:source.

Revill, G. (1993) 'Reading Rosehill: Community, Identity and Inner-city Derby' in M. Keith and S. Pile (eds.), *Place and the Politics of Identity*. London, Routledge, 117–37.

Richardson, N. L. (1997) *Education for Mutual Understanding and Cultural Heritage*. Available at http://cain.ulst.ac.uk/emu/emuback.htm, accessed February 2003.

Rolston, B. (1998) 'What's Wrong with Multiculturalism? Liberalism and the Irish Conflict' in D. Miller (ed.), *Rethinking Northern Ireland: Culture, Ideology and Colonialism*. London and New York, Longman.

Ruiz, J. (2004) *A Literature Review of the Evidence Base for Culture, the Arts and Social Policy*. Edinburgh, Education Department Research Programme Scottish Executive.

Saguaro Seminar (2000) *Better Together. The Report of the Saguaro Seminar: Civic Engagement in America*. Available at http://www.bettertogether.org/thereport.htm.

Sandell, R. (1998) 'Museums as Agents of Social Inclusion'. *Museum Management and Curatorship* 17 (4), 401–18.

—— (ed.) (2002) *Museums, Society, Inequality*. London, Routledge.

Schofield, B. (2002) 'Partners in Power: Governing the Self-sustaining Community'. *Sociology* 36 (3), 663–83.

Schuller, T., S. Baron and J. Field (2000) 'Social Capital: A Review and Critique' in Baron *et al.* 2000, 1–38.

Scott, A. (1995) *Ideology and the New Social Movements*. London, Routledge.

Scottish Executive (2002) *Scotland's National Cultural Strategy Annual Report*. Edinburgh, Scottish Executive.

Scottish Museums Council (2000) *Museums and Social Justice*. Edinburgh, SMC.

—— (2005) *A National Learning and Access Strategy for Museums and Galleries in Scotland*. Edinburgh, SMC.

Sharrock, G. (2006) 'Beads, Bugs and Tea: Community Learning Programs'. Paper presented at Museums Australia National Conference *Exploring Dynamics: Cities, Cultural Spaces, Communities*. Available at www.museumsaustralia.org, accessed 7 June 2006.

Shaw, L. (2004) *Changing the Culture of Museums and Galleries: Creating a More Diverse Workforce. Diversify Evaluation Report*. London, Museums Association.

Simpson, M. G. (2006) 'Revealing and Concealing: Museums, Objects and the Transmission of Knowledge in Aborginal Australia' in J. Marstine (ed.), *New Museum Theory and Practice: An Introduction*. Oxford, Blackwell, 152–74.

Sklenar, K. (1983) *Archaeology in Central Europe: The Last Five Hundred Years*. Leicester, Leicester University Press.

Smith, A. D. (1991) *National Identity*. London, Penguin.

Smith, A. and A. Robinson (1992) *Education for Mutual Understanding: Perceptions and Policy*. Centre for the Study of Conflict, University of Ulster.

—— (1996) *Education for Mutual Understanding: The Initial Statutory Years*. Centre for the Study of Conflict, University of Ulster.

Social Exclusion Unit (1998) *Bringing Britain Together: A National Strategy for Neighbourhood Renewal*. London: Social Exclusion Unit.

Somers Cocks, A. (2003) 'Is Cultural Diversity Good for the Arts? Diversity in Difficult Times'. *Spiked* 17 June.

Soudien, C. (2001) 'The First Few Years of the District Six Museum Foundation' in Rassool and Prosalendis 2001, 5–6.

South East England Museum, Library and Archive Council (2004) *Guidance Sheets on Cultural Diversity* (nos. 1–9). Winchester, SEMLAC.

—— (2005) *Social Inclusion Strategy 2005–2007*. Winchester, SEMLAC.

Strickson, K. (2004) *Stories in a Suitcase: Looking Back and Looking Forward with the People of Ravensthorpe*. Kirklees, Kirklees Metropolitan Council.

Taylor, C. (1994) *Multiculturalism: Examining the Politics of Recognition*. Princeton, Princeton University Press.

Todd, M. J. and G. Taylor (eds.) (2004) *Democracy and Participation: Popular Protest and New Social Movements*. London, The Merlin Press.

Tower Museum, Education Department, Derry City Council (2004–5) Papers in connection with the development of Good Relations Programme. Unpublished.

Ulster People's College (2000) Grant application for European Social Funds 2000–4 Measure 2.1 Reconciliation for Sustainable Peace (application made by UPC to fund and support the People's History Initiative). Unpublished.

—— (2000–5) People's History Initiative Project: Reports submitted to Community Relations Council EU Programme for Peace and Reconciliation Measure 2.1 Reconciliation for Sustainable Peace (including reports for Sept 2002–June 2003; July 2003–December 2003; January 2004–June 2004; July 2004–December 2004; January 2005–June 2005). Unpublished.

—— (2002) *Prospectus*. Belfast, UPC.

—— (2003) *Shared Future: A Response from Ulster People's College*. 30 September. Available at http://www.asharedfutureni.gov.uk.

Ulster Folk and Transport Museum (2006) Education Department, Evaluation of Community Relations Programmes, feedback from students and teachers attending workshops. Unpublished internal documents.

UNESCO (2002) *Universal Declaration on Cultural Diversity*. Paris, UNESCO. Available at www.unesco.org/culture.

—— (2005) *Convention on the Protection and Promotion of the Diversity of Cultural Expressions*. Paris, UNESCO.

Van der Veen, R. (2003) 'Community Development as Citizen Education'. *International Journal of Lifelong Education* 22 (6), 580–96.

Verma, J. (2003) 'Is Cultural Diversity Good for the Arts? No'. *Spiked* 9 June.

Weil, S. (1998) 'The Museum and the Public'. *Museum Management and Curatorship* 16 (3), 257–71.

West, P. (2005) *The Poverty of Multiculturalism*. London, Civitas: Institute for the Study of Civil Society.

Women into Irish History (2002) *'Sure What Did We Know About It'*. Londonderry, Shared City Initiative, Waterside Museum.

Wood, C. and H. Gould (2005) *Culture Shock: Tolerance, Respect, Understanding . . . and Museums*. Truro, Campaign for Learning in Museums and Galleries.

Young, L. (2005) *Our Lives, Our Histories, Our Collections*. London, Museum of London.

Websites consulted

American Association of Museums. Section on Museums and Community Initiative. www.aam-us.org/initiatives/m&c/, accessed April 2003.

Commission for Racial Equality. www.cre.gov.uk/legal/rra_positive.html, accessed 26 October 2006.

Community Archiving Network, Northern Ireland. www.canni.net, accessed September 2006.

Community Development Xchange (CDX). www.cdx.org.uk, accessed 15 August 2005.

Department of Culture, Arts and Leisure (Northern Ireland). Section on *New Targeting Social Need*. www.dcalni.gov.uk/ContMan/includes/upload/file.asp?ContentID=454&file=c_23.

Department for Culture, Media and Sport, UK. www.culture.gov.uk, section on strategic objectives, accessed 28 June 2006.

Department for Victorian Communities, Australia. www.dvc.vic.gov.au, accessed August 2005.

District Six Museum. www.districtsix.co.za, accessed March 2001.

Eastern England Museums, Libraries and Archives Council, section on cultural diversity. www.eemlac.co.uk, accessed February 2003.

Fermanagh Trust, Northern Ireland. Section on community groups. www.fermanaghtrust.org, accessed 18 May 2004.

Glasgow Museums. Section on open museum. www.glasgow.gov.uk, accessed 29 September 2006.

Government of New South Wales, Australia. www.communitybuilders.nsw.gov.au, accessed 23 August 2005.

Home Office, UK. www.homeoffice.gov.uk: Section on community cohesion, accessed 2 September 2005; Section on civil renewal unit, accessed 17 October 2005.

House of Commons, UK *Hansard*. www.publications.parliament.uk, accessed 26 August 2006.

Institute of Ideas. www.instituteofideas.com.

International Council of Museums: Section on *Code of Ethics*. http://icom.museum/code2006_eng.pdf. Section on cultural diversity http://icom.museum/diversity.html, last accessed 5 October 2006.

Migration Heritage Centre, Australia. http://migrationheritage.nsw.gov.au, accessed 23 August 2005.

Ministry of Culture, Ontario. www.culture.gov.on.ca, accessed 21 November 2005.

Museum of London. Section on The Reassessing What We Collect Project. www.museumoflondon.org.uk, accessed 10 August 2006.

Museums Association, UK. Section on Diversify! Initiative. www.museumsassociation.org, accessed 26 October 2006.

Museums Australia Cultural Diversity Strategy. www.museumsaustralia.org.au, accessed February 2003.

Museums, Libraries and Archives Council, UK. Section on Sustainable Communities Summit. www.mla.gov.uk, accessed September 2005.

National Council on Archives. www.ncaonline.org.uk, accessed 26 September 2006.

North East Museums, Libraries and Archives Council. www.nemlac.co.uk/strategy.htm, accessed 7 November 2005.

North West Museums Service, UK. Section on cultural diversity. www.nwmuseums.co.uk, accessed February 2003.

Northern Ireland Assembly. Section on Deprivation Index. www.niassembly.gov.uk/io/research/0202.pdf.

Northern Ireland Museums Council. www.nimc.co.uk.

Nova Scotia Department of Tourism, Culture and Heritage. www.gov.ns.ca/dtc, accessed 23 May 2006.

Office of the Deputy Prime Minister, UK. Section on communities. www.odpm.gov.uk.

Office of the First Minister and Deputy First Minister, Northern Ireland. Section on *A Shared Future*. www.asharedfutureni.gov.uk.

Oral History Society, UK. www.ohs.org.uk, accessed 16 September 2005.

Regeneration of South Armagh, Northern Ireland. Section on heritage maps. www.rosa.ie, accessed October 2006.

Re:source, UK. www.resource.gov.uk.

Saguaro Seminar, US. www.ksg.harvard.ed/saguaro.

Scottish Museums Council. www.smc.co.uk.

South East England Museum, Library and Archive Council. www.semlac.org.uk.

Spiked. Section on Culture and Difference. www.spiked-online.com/Sections/Culture/debates/CulturalDiversity, accessed 31 July 2006.

Ulster Folk and Transport Museum. Section on community relations. www.uftm.org.uk/learning/Community_Relations, accessed 10 July 2006.

Index

NOTE: Page numbers in **bold** type refer to an illustration.